Blessed Connections

Relationships That Sustain Vital Ministry

Judith A. Schwanz

THE
ALBAN
INSTITUTE

Herndon, Virginia
www.alban.org

The Alban Institute
2121 Cooperative Way, Suite 100
Herndon, VA 20171

Cover design by Signal Hill.

Library of Congress Cataloging-in-Publication Data

Schwanz, Judith A.
    Blessed connections : relationships that sustain vital ministry / Judith A. Schwanz.
        p. cm.
    Includes bibliographical references.
    ISBN 978-1-56699-356-2
    1. Pastoral theology. 2. Clergy. 3. Interpersonal relations--Religious aspects--Christianity. I. Title.

BV4011.3.S39 2008
253'.2--dc22
                                        2008002528

    12   11   10   09   08   VP   1   2   3   4   5

Contents

119501

Foreword

For the past seven years, I have been coordinating Lilly Endowment's Transition into Ministry program. In this program we
have been learning a great deal about what makes for a successful
transition from the training for ministry in the academic setting to
the practice of ministry in the congregational setting. Through the
various programs funded in this project and the several hundred
beginning pastors who have participated in them, we have become
convinced that one of the best predictors of success in ministry
is what Judith Schwanz has named, "the relational system of the
minister's life." Understanding the importance of relationships
and attending appropriately to the cultivation of strong relational
capacities is at the heart of successful ministry.

All too often reflection on the relational life of a pastor fails
to appreciate the unique context of congregational life. Unlike
many other professions where clients are seen in an office setting
or within a narrow band of life experience, the pastor functions
in an environment in which the office is only one space—a minor
one at that—where encounters with parishioners occur. A pastor
engages his or her parishioners in a variety of settings across the
whole range of life experience. If guidance on the relational life of

the pastor is to be wise, it must be rooted in an appreciation for the unique character of congregational life and practice.

With her thirty years of pastoral experience, Judith Schwanz understands the promise and the perils intrinsic to congregational life and leadership. She draws upon a wide variety of resources—biblical, theological, sociological, and psychological—to map the relational challenges of pastoral ministry. At the heart of her analysis and guidance are her first-hand knowledge of ecclesial reality and her abiding appreciation of the unique challenges and opportunities for relationships that reality provides.

Schwanz understands that while pastoral practice entails a fairly predictable range of functions and corresponding skills, how an individual pastor embodies that practice is infinitely variable. Appreciating both the constancy of pastoral practice (and the discipline it requires of all its inhabitants) and the particular set of gifts and capacities of each pastor (and the creativity and improvisation they make possible) is a conviction that informs almost every page of this book. The most effective pastors are those who flourish as persons through their work. Such flourishing depends as much upon a healthy self-awareness as it does upon a faithful commitment to the work of ministry. The process Schwanz invites the reader into is designed to cultivate an understanding of self and of ministry that will provide a rich context for integrating the role of the pastor with the person of the pastor.

One final note to the reader: My sense is that this book is best read in the company of others—in particular, in the company of peers in ministry. My hunch is that working through a book like this together will go a long way towards generating the kind of 'blessed connections' Judith Schwanz rightly regards as being so critical to excellence in ministry.

David J. Wood
Coordinator of Lilly Endowment's
Transition into Ministry Program

Preface

I love the church. The church has been an integral part of my life as long as I can remember. Other than my hospital newborn photos, the earliest pictures I have ever seen of myself were taken with my mother and father in the church nursery. We rarely missed a service. My parents were very active laypeople, serving in a variety of ministries until age and illness finally made them resign. I guess it's in my DNA.

When I say that I love the church, I really don't mean the building where I go to worship each week. I mean the people that gather each week to worship God together, the people who make up the family of faith. The church became my family. Both my parents were only children, and my father's parents both had died by the time my parents were married. In the church I found aunts and uncles and additional grandparents.

I even met my husband in church. Our first home was the parish house of the church where Keith was the youth pastor and choir director. We have both given our adult lives to full-time ministry in service to the church.

Because I love the church, I want to see the people who make up the church become all that God intended them to be.

God has enriched my life through relationships—in my family, in the church, and in my relationship with God. I am convinced that healthy relationships help build healthy pastors and healthy congregations.

In more than thirty years of ministry, including two years on staff in a Christian inpatient psychiatric unit, I have seen that church systems sometimes bring more pain than healing. Relationships that should bring blessing, instead sometimes end in division and lead to isolation.

This book is my message to pastors. Your journey through these pages will guide you to a deeper understanding of yourself as God created you and to deepening relationships with other people and with God.

I have told many stories throughout this book. Some of them are my own, my husband's, and my children's. The other stories come from students and ministry colleagues through whom God has blessed my life. If the name in a story is followed by an asterisk* I have either chosen a fictional name to protect someone's confidence or I have combined details from two or more specific stories to simplify the telling of the tale. Unless otherwise noted, I have used the Today's New International Version (TNIV) of Scripture.

As you read, I hope that you will also keep an Assessment Journal. When you respond to the questions in each chapter, you will be writing your own story. I pray that you will discover anew the life-giving power of your connection with yourself, with others, and with God.

Introduction

Ministry for Life

As I sit on the platform at yet another seminary graduation, my heart overflows. The sight of students marching one-by-one past the podium to receive their diplomas and have their hoods draped over their robed shoulders brings a flood of memories. We have shared classes and meals together. We have wrestled with difficult concepts and distilled case studies.

Having responded to God's call, these women and men have worked hard, investing years of their lives to develop the gifts that God has given them. These students are prepared for the ministries that await them. Some already have church positions. Others will leave this week, moving into unknown territories, new parts of the country, unfamiliar parsonages. Some will be heading to other countries, even dangerous situations. I rejoice with them in the new adventure. I look forward to hearing stories of spiritual victories and the joys of ministry.

Yet, in the corner of my mind, a fearful voice reminds me of a frightening reality. I can't help but remember the one who, years before, joyously celebrated a seminary graduation and today has lost his family in the wake of an affair with a parishioner. Or the woman who moved to her first pastorate with stars in her eyes and this year resigned that church after being questioned one too many times about her "right" to preach.

As I look at the group of graduates, I recall the statistics: 15 to 20 percent of pastors leave pastoral ministry within the first five years of ministry. Clergy marriages fare little better than the national average of marriages ending in divorce. Which of this group of graduates will make it in ministry and marriage for the long term?

No pastor sets out to fail. Most of us want to be the best we can be in whatever we undertake. On graduation day, of all days, no one wants to consider the possibility of failure or disillusionment. Every minister wants to be an effective pastor and rest in the assurance of God's affirmation, "Well done, good and faithful servant."

But, in fact, countless pastors leave the ministry discouraged, disillusioned, and defeated. H. B. London and Neil Wiseman reported on a study that revealed 50 percent of pastors said they felt unable to meet the needs of the job, 90 percent felt inadequately trained to cope with ministry demands, and 70 percent said their self-esteem was lower now than when they first started in ministry.[1] These findings and the symptoms they describe are often labeled "ministry burnout." In the last few decades numerous books and articles have been written on clergy burnout. Most of these take one of three approaches: definition/diagnosis, addressing role causes, or addressing a single cause.

The Definition Approach to Clergy Burnout

Many researchers and writers have sought to define burnout in order to help clergy catch it in the early stages and take preemptive action for renewal. This approach focuses on building awareness of warning signs, raising red flags that indicate the individual needs to find a source of renewal.

In social science research, the most widely accepted model of burnout is presented by Christina Maslach.[2] She identified three major factors of burnout among those in the helping professions: (1) increased emotional exhaustion, (2) increased depersonalization of the people receiving one's care, and (3) a decreased sense of personal accomplishment. She developed an inventory to measure these factors, but declined to establish cutoff scores at which point one could say, "I *am* [or am not] burned out." She conceptualized burnout on a continuum. Her focus was on identifying warning signs and encouraging individuals to make the necessary life changes to decrease the levels of these three factors in their lives.

My own research applied Maslach's model to those in pastoral ministry. Seventy percent of those responding reported moderate to high levels of emotional exhaustion.[3] Forty percent acknowledged a moderate to high level of depersonalization. This means that they began to see the people with whom they ministered as objects, not people with names and identities. For example, Sister Smith has become "the old biddy who sits on the back row and complains she can't hear."

A significant percentage of the pastors (25 percent) in this study also showed a diminished sense of personal accomplishment. However, a significant number of pastors scored high on the other two factors but not on lowered personal accomplishment. In their answers to the open-ended questions, these pastors all talked about call and about feelings of failure in their ministry. Although they didn't necessarily perceive their ministries as effective, they *did* perceive that they were doing God's work and following God's call; therefore, they were accomplishing something.

This study certainly confirmed high levels of these burnout factors among pastors, but the church must move beyond identification to proactive prevention. While understanding the components of burnout and having a working definition are helpful, this approach is not enough. We must explore causes of burnout and suggest ways to ameliorate those causes.

The Role Causes Approach to Clergy Burnout

John Sanford is a pastoral counselor who addressed the issue
of burnout from the perspective of the special circumstances of
ministry that enhance a pastor's vulnerability to burnout.[4] One
of the most negative circumstances has to do with difficult people
in the church. Numerous books have been written about those
who criticize, attack, and undermine leadership in the church and
how the minister can best deal with them to avoid burnout and
total defeat. Titles like *The Wounded Minister*, *Never Call Them
Jerks*, *Antagonists in the Church*, and *Clergy Killers* clearly reveal
the content of the books. The authors of these books seek to help
pastors survive in the face of painful opposition and occasional
outright attack.[5]

The Single Cause Approach to Clergy Burnout

Yet other writers have hailed one precursor as a key issue and addressed that concern. Dan Spaite focused on the minister's need
for Sabbath renewal.[6] Ray Anderson asserted that burnout is a
symptom of theological anemia.[7] Gary Kinnaman and Alfred Ells
identified isolation as the key issue and maintained that covenant
friendships with other pastors allow the minister to weather difficult times without succumbing to burnout.[8]

A New Way: A Systemic
Relational Approach to Clergy Burnout

Many of these resources are excellent. I have included a fairly ex-
tensive list of them in the bibliography. I have read them eagerly
in my desire to help the pastors with whom I work—both students

and clergy colleagues. But the solutions offered feel at times like first aid administered too late, after the injury. Each analysis deals with part of the problem but not the root. Or they feel external, like something we do, rather than focusing on who we *are*. This can result in improvement, but often the solution and results are temporary and burnout recurs.

Burnout in the ministry is a complex phenomenon. No one answer will provide a cure-all. Each person and each ministry situation is unique. A comprehensive, proactive approach is needed that focuses on the many facets of clergy health and the prevention of clergy burnout.

This book focuses on the person of the minister and the relational system of the minister's life. Specifically, three areas of connection will be considered—relationship with self, relationships with other people, and relationship with God. Attending to these three primary connections strengthens the pastor and cushions her or him against the pressures and stresses of daily ministry. Relationships bring vitality and life to daily human existence. Relationships also bring longevity; they sustain us over time, enhancing the likelihood that we will not only survive but thrive over the long term. Connection brings life.

Clergy cannot escape relationships in their ministry. A seminary administrator once told me that every person he had heard of leaving the ministry had done so because of a relationship failure. Yet, few seminaries offer courses in how to build healthy relationships. Current studies in business leadership indicate the importance of emotional intelligence for success in any leadership position. Peter Salovey and John D. Mayer coined the term *emotional intelligence* (EI) in 1990. They defined EI as "a form of social intelligence that involves the ability to monitor one's own and others' feelings and emotions, to discriminate among them, and to use this information to guide one's thinking and action."[9]

Churchgoers tend to assume that the type of person who is called to ministry has all the people skills he or she needs, but, sadly, that is not true. I have had students tell me in moments of honesty, "I really don't like working with people. If I could just stay in my office most of the time and study, pray, and prepare my sermons, I'd be happy."

Daniel Goleman identified four primary domains of emotional intelligence: (1) self-awareness, (2) self-management, (3) social awareness, and (4) relationship management.[10] In the next chapter, you and I will consider how self-awareness and self-management are key aspects of authenticity. Awareness of others and the ability to manage our relationships with others affects the way in which we connect. We will consider those issues in later chapters.

Goleman and his associates studied businesses around the world and the various leaders at different levels of those businesses.[11] Their research revealed the painful consequences of leadership without emotional intelligence. For employees, such leadership often resulted in low morale, lowered productivity, and increased employee conflict and turnover. A leader without emotional intelligence often experiences failure and frustration.

A pastoral leader without emotional intelligence will experience the same feelings of failure and frustration. Over time, a congregation led by an emotionally unskilled pastor will likely experience high turnover (an active "back door" syndrome), low morale, and increased conflict.

The converse also seems to be true. Emotionally intelligent pastors experience higher morale and less frequent, less intense conflict among their people. Chad Johnson explored the relationship between emotional intelligence and pastoral leadership.[12] He suggested that leaders with strong relational capacities empower their followers to be faithful, available, teachable, honest, open, and transparent.

Books on leadership for the business community may address relationships with self and others but generally do not consider the leader's relationship with God. The unique nature of pastoral leadership implicitly requires a healthy relationship with God. Jesus told the disciples, "I am the vine; you are the branches . . . apart from me you can do nothing" (John 15:5 NIV). The pastoral effectiveness of the one called to ministry must be directly related to his or her relationship with the One who calls.

Connected for Life

A systemic relational approach considers all of the relationships in a pastor's life. This book consists of three major sections. In the first major section, chapters 1 through 3, we will consider what it means to have a healthy self-understanding—that is, knowing one's strengths and growing edges, spiritual gifts, and vulnerabilities. We will also explore the importance of living out of our authentic selves rather than attempting to project an ideal image, which leads to burnout.

In the second section, chapters 4 through 7, we will focus on building strong interpersonal relationships with spouse, children, and friends as well as with members of the congregations and the larger community in which the pastor lives.

In the third section, chapters 8 through 11, we will address the pastor's need for a deep and sustaining relationship with God that provides inner strength and pervading peace with which to face the dark days and heavy burdens of ministry when they come.

Each chapter includes guidelines for developing and using an Assessment Journal to accurately reflect on present relationships and for developing a Personal and Professional Growth Plan.

Becoming the very best pastor you can be begins with the journey of self-discovery. So, let's explore together what it means to truly know yourself, to value your strengths, and to be open to growth in all areas of your life.

1

Truly Authentic

Your Relationship with Yourself

"Get real!" "He's the real deal!"

So many people today worry about their public image. Some even hire image consultants. Makeovers abound—home, wardrobe, cosmetics, and every other imaginable effort toward perfection. Hollywood reporters tell us that high-definition television has celebrities worried because the high clarity makes it difficult to mask flaws that makeup artists can hide on nondigital television. Images wear thin after a while. In real life we are not airbrushed to cover blemishes. We don't have the chance for repeated takes in our interactions with others. We may even begin to wonder what we *can* believe. We listen to news reports somewhat skeptically, wondering what spin has been given to the facts. We long for the unvarnished truth. We admire people who are real, where what you see is what you get.

How well do you know yourself? How well do you like the self you know? For long-term ministry, pastors need to be authentic—that is, to know their strengths and weaknesses and to understand and accept themselves as they are.

When was the last time you went shopping for a new pair of jeans? Being authentic is like finding the perfect pair of jeans. For years, as a short person, I have hemmed too-long new denims and endured waistbands that didn't land in the right place. I have watched other people parade in front of dressing room mirrors, holding in their breath, as well as their tummies, saying, "But I've always worn a size 8!" Fear of admitting figure flaws may keep them in clothing so tight they can't sit down or bend over.

What joy I experienced the first time I walked into a store that sold pants by waist and inseam measurements and in several degrees of fit or tightness. I experienced new levels of comfort as I wore jeans that truly fit *me*. This joy is nothing compared to the joy and freedom that comes as pastors shape ministry patterns that fit them uniquely.

We must make a conscious choice to become authentic, to "take our measurements," if you will. Ironically, becoming authentic does not come naturally because most of us have been programmed by our families or our society to try to be something or someone we are not. Some of us have been handed a script by our family of origin or by other significant people in our lives and expected to play a role.

Experts in the field of emotional intelligence and leadership identify self-awareness as the first domain or skill necessary for effective leaders. Self-knowledge is essential to authenticity. I cannot be the real me if I don't know who I am "warts and all," as my mother used to say.

All of us function at our best when we discover who we really are. This process of discovery is like a treasure hunt as we seek to know our strengths, weaknesses, gifts, and vulnerabilities. Only when we truly know ourselves can we fully develop the next domain of emotional intelligence, which is managing ourselves. Self-management implies self-control and adaptability, which allow us to use our gifts and strengths to the best advantage and to control our weaknesses. The pastor who knows himself and has learned to manage himself is truly authentic.

Chad Johnson observed that emotionally intelligent leaders know themselves and lead with transparency. This means that "they are genuine in their desire to serve others, they are interested in empowering the people they lead, they are guided by the qualities of the heart and mind, and those who work with or follow them can see this authenticity coming through in everything they do."[1]

Imitation: Flattery or Phoniness?

A recent seminary graduate, John came back to visit after a year in his first church. He sat in my office looking totally dejected. "I'm exhausted! Ministry is harder than anyone ever told me it would be! I can't do this any longer." He drilled down to the source of his pain when he added, "I can never be the kind of pastor Everett is."

Young pastors are especially vulnerable to this kind of frustration, particularly in their first assignment. John idolized Everett, who still pastored the church where John grew up. When John first sensed God calling him to pastoral ministry, he talked to his beloved pastor and asked him to be his mentor. He knew he wanted to be just like Everett when he, too, became a pastor.

The problem was that John and Everett were *very* different men. They had different gifts and interests. John could not become his mentor's clone no matter how hard he tried. What energized Everett exhausted or bored John, and the aspects of ministry that Everett dreaded were those that John found exhilarating. John needed to discover himself so he could be the best Pastor John possible.

We all have our Everetts—someone we have said we want to grow up to be like. Mentors and role models can help us and challenge us to grow, shaping our values and interests. The danger comes when we try to become exact replicas of our models. As a seminary student, I researched the life and work of Mother Teresa. I deeply admire her and respect the work of the Missionaries of Charity. I don't expect that I will ever do the work she has done or be just like her. But whenever I think of her, I am inspired and reminded of *my* responsibility to the poor in *my* community.

Throughout the New Testament the only model the faithful are called to imitate is God. We are not instructed to copy a specific behavior or personality style but to imitate God by living a life of love. Paul's directions in the epistles to imitate *him* challenge the reader to imitate his way of life *in Christ Jesus* (1 Cor. 4:14-17). He congratulated the Thessalonian believers for imitating his faithfulness in persecution (1 Thess. 1:6; 2:14).

Thus, I am called to imitate Christ by loving God and loving others. I seek to be the best Jesus follower I can be—within my own body, in my own unique way. Francis de Sales, a sixteenth and seventeenth century Roman Catholic bishop, encouraged his followers to "Be who you are and be it well that you may bring honor to the Master Craftsman whose handiwork you are."

Authenticity—the Benefits

Authenticity, becoming the "genuine article," has several benefits—we can relax and be our best selves, we are less likely to be blindsided by emotional baggage, and we are far less vulnerable to burnout.

We Can Relax

The most significant benefit is that when we are authentic, we can let down our guard; we don't need to try to copy our ideal, but we can be ourselves. For many years as a pastor's wife, I carried in my wallet a cartoon cut from a magazine. Two women were standing beside a giant pair of high-heeled pumps big enough for the Old Woman Who Lived in a Shoe. One woman pointed to the shoes and said, "These belonged to our former pastor's wife. Can you fill them?"

Many pastors and pastors' spouses accept the challenge to fill someone else's shoes as part of God's call. But when we try to be someone we are not, we live a lie. A wise woman I know often paraphrases Mark Twain: "If you tell the truth, you don't have to remember what you said. If you lie, it's too hard to remember your story." Living authentically allows us to throw away our scripts, forget about memorizing lines, and relax. God asks us to fill our *own* shoes, not someone else's.

We Can Be Our Best Selves

We can set manageable goals and make greater progress when we have an accurate assessment of our current condition. Gordon MacDonald challenges pastors to take an "inner tour" of themselves, which involves an accounting of their emotions, and an "outer tour" of their personalities, strengths, and weaknesses.[2] When I quit worrying about being what I am not, I can focus on building on my strengths.

Family systems theorists have introduced the concept of differentiation, which is related, in part, to authenticity. The differentiated person remains in a system of relationships, but maintains her own identity and sense of self without getting lost in the system. Differentiation will be more deeply explored in future chapters where I talk about relationships with others. As we consider authenticity, each person needs to understand that differentiation involves knowing "what I am" and "what I am not." With this knowledge, each of us can focus on developing what we are and not waste energy trying to be what we are not.

We Are Less Likely to Be Blindsided by Emotional Baggage

When we embark on what MacDonald called an inner tour through our past personal history, we reap another benefit. As we see ourselves more deeply and honestly, we discover those areas of emotional pain, of unresolved hurts or questions. We know our own tender spots, those sources of anger, injury, or unforgiveness. This may not sound like a benefit at first, but once we are aware of past issues, we can deal with them and move on more freely without their weight.

Joseph Luft and Harry Ingram developed a model called the Johari Window to illustrate relationships in terms of self- and other-awareness (see Figure 1.1).[3] Each pane or quadrant in the diagram represents a collection of knowledge about the individual, which includes factual information, such as name and physical appearance, and also feelings, motivations, behaviors, needs, desires, and attitudes. The "open" quadrant represents things that we know about ourselves and that other people also know about us. The "blind" quadrant includes those things that others can see in us of which we are unaware. The "hidden," or avoided, quadrant consists of those things we know about ourselves but don't allow others to see, and the "unknown" quadrant includes those things about ourselves of which we and others are unaware, which have not yet been discovered.

	Known to Self	Unknown to Self
Known to Others	Open Pane: known to self and others	Blind Pane: blind to self, seen by others
Unknown to Others	Hidden Pane: open to self, hidden from others	Unknown Pane: unknown to self and others

Figure 1.1. Johari Window

We will explore this model in more detail in the next chapter, looking at how to discover and measure our strengths and weaknesses. For now, it is enough to say that we want to increase the open and hidden quadrants, allowing us to see ourselves more clearly, and we want to decrease the blind and unknown portions of our being.

Numerous training programs for professional counselors see the need for this inner tour and require students to undergo their own personal counseling. Some students are drawn to the field of counseling because they themselves have been hurt in some way and want to help others avoid the pain they experienced or they have benefited from counseling and want to offer the same help to others. The same is true of many men and women called to pastoral ministry, which is the basic premise of Henri Nouwen's classic book, *The Wounded Healer*.[4] Becoming aware of and owning your emotional baggage is the essential first step to breaking the power of the past over your present. Authenticity requires acknowledging your wounds and nondefensively taking the necessary steps toward healing. Thus, becoming authentic is directly related to emotional health and wholeness.

We Are Less Vulnerable to Burnout

When we are authentic and differentiated, we are far less vulnerable to burnout. Let's consider Maslach's three factors of burnout to see the connection with authenticity.

The first factor is increased *emotional exhaustion*. My family recently took a trip to Hawaii. My favorite "activity" was sitting on the lanai with a book on my lap, sipping chocolate macadamia nut coffee. From my comfortable perch, I listened to the surf and watched the waves crash on the sand and rocks in its constant motion.

On occasion, I ventured to the beach and the water. My daughter and I would lie on our boogie boards and float, chatting lazily while we enjoyed the gentle tug and push of the waves and the sun on our backs. Every so often one of us would look around and notice how far we had been moved down the shore. The tide had pulled us without our being aware of it. We would have to turn and paddle back to where we could see our towels in the sand. The paddling against the current took much more energy than floating with the tide. If I had chosen to paddle against the tide all day I would have become exhausted.

The pastor who is trying to follow a script or someone else's pattern for ministry expends a lot of energy, going against the tide of her own personal best pattern. Emotional exhaustion almost certainly will result when she tries to be someone she is not.

Instead, when the pastor discovers his own inner source of drive (or tide) and works *with* it, he will cease fighting himself and will find ministry doesn't take so much energy. He will be much less prone to emotional exhaustion.

The second factor of Maslach's model of burnout is an increased tendency toward *depersonalization*. In my experience, when I focus on living up to an image or on trying to be someone that I know I "should" be, I tend to expect the same from others. This causes me to see people as objects, often either as hindrances or means to my own ends. Objects don't have names or needs.

When I see myself as a real person, admitting my defeats as well as my successes and owning who I am, I am much more likely to see other people that way, too. Authenticity is a weapon against the tendency to depersonalize those whom God has entrusted to our care.

Maslach's third factor is a decreased sense of *personal accomplishment*. My son, Jason, *loves* sports. As a sixth grader, he participated in every athletic team available: basketball, cross country, wrestling, track, and baseball. Like many boys his age, he covered the walls of his bedroom with posters of his favorite players. He seemed especially drawn to basketball, as we were living in Portland, Oregon, in the days when the Trailblazers were especially fun to watch. We put up a basketball hoop in the back yard and he practiced for hours.

However, his team's games often left him disappointed, as he spent a lot of time on the bench. One of the shortest boys in his class, Jason seemed at a convenient level for his eyes to connect with the opponents' elbows. In one game he broke two pairs of glasses! He knew he would never be a star player or fulfill his dream of being a pro, but he did love the game. He expended a lot of energy and didn't feel he accomplished much. This was a perfect environment for him to develop burnout.

But when he discovered wrestling, it was a different matter. He wrestled in the lowest weight class his freshman year and did very well. On the wrestling mat, his size and build were matched with those of his opponent.

He experienced a much greater sense of accomplishment when he found the sport that fit him. He earned the ribbons, the certificates, and a varsity letter each of four years to prove it. He channeled his energy in that arena in which he fit and could excel, going with the tide of his body rather than trying to be someone he was not.

Pastors who know their strengths and accept their limitations experience a similarly higher sense of personal accomplishment in ministry. This increased sense of accomplishment comes from two sources. The first source is the sheer fact that such a pastor truly *does* accomplish more, just as a swimmer or boater going with the tide covers more distance than the person going against the tide. Not only does the pastor accomplish more but also she uses less energy in the process, so at the end of the day, she has an emotional reserve.

The second source of the feeling of accomplishment has to do with expectations and valuing what is accomplished. Today Jason could join in a pick-up basketball game and play hard. At the end he might say, "Well, I made a good shot or two and had fun," and that would be enough. As an adult, he no longer wrestles, but his experience in sports has taught him to look for and develop his areas of strength at work and at play.

So, according to Maslach's three-factor model, authenticity lowers our vulnerability to burnout. Parker Palmer pointed out the energizing results of being real: "When the gift I give to the other is integral to my own nature, when it comes from a place of organic reality within me, it will renew itself—and me—even as I give it away. Only when I give something that does not grow within me do I deplete myself and harm the other as well, for only harm can come from a gift that is forced, inorganic, unreal."[5]

That which energizes us minimizes the tendency toward burnout.

Authenticity—the Costs

You have probably already sensed that being authentic has risks. In the children's story *The Velveteen Rabbit*, the toys learned that becoming real can be a painful experience. To be truly honest with ourselves, before we embark on the search for our real selves, we need to count the costs as well as the benefits.

We May Face Rejection

Perhaps the most obvious risk of honesty and transparency is rejection. In my counseling work, I have heard people in all walks of life say, "If people knew the real me, they wouldn't like me." They feel like fakes, but they won't risk rejection. People in positions of authority may fear authenticity because they are afraid people won't trust them or follow their leadership if their failures are known. Sometimes parents refuse to admit to their children that they were wrong because they fear their children will no longer respect them. So they keep up a facade, pretending they have it all together.

The truth is that some people may reject us. Usually, those are folks with extremely high and rigid standards. We may never measure up in their books, anyway, so we might as well relax and be our best selves. Family systems theory presents the concept of differentiation as the ability of persons to remain connected to others yet maintain their own identity. The well-differentiated individual cares about others but is not controlled by their expectations or driven to please them. Differentiation allows you to say to those who disapprove of you, "I wish you would accept me as I am. I am trying my best to follow the example of Jesus. I'm sorry that I disappoint you, but I cannot live up to the expectations that you have for me."

A second reason that we might face rejection is that our own authenticity may cause others to sense the roles they play by contrast. Our freedom may make them uncomfortable, because they aren't ready to take the risk. For example, I led a Bible study where Joan* admitted that she struggled with anger. She asked the group to pray for her to have more patience with her two preschool children, whom she feared she might hurt in a moment of rage. The group was silent after her request, unsure of how to respond. I noticed over the next few weeks that a number of women no longer talked about their children or parenting issues in the group. Fortunately, as others continue to watch our authentic lives, perhaps from a safe emotional distance, they may be drawn into their own process of self-discovery and authenticity. In this group, after a few weeks, others ventured to tell of their frustrations as young mothers and to help each other as they shared how they each dealt with their own anger.

As we get to know ourselves better and let others see our real selves, we begin to develop a sixth sense about who we can trust with our vulnerabilities and who we should not trust. Some people seem to be born with that sixth sense intact and others have had it severely damaged on the road to adulthood.

"TMI"—too much information. I learned this phrase from my children when they were in high school. I have seen this concept in action with a few of my adult students.

Marcie* is a beautiful woman with a sweet spirit. She is also a walking testimony of God's grace. No one who meets her for the first time would ever guess the horrible years of abuse she endured, first at the hands of her parents and then with a violent husband. As a child she learned to trust no one. Her marriage reinforced that lesson.

Marcie encountered a God who loved her and she put her trust in Jesus. Over time she also developed relationships with caring Christians who accepted her in ways she had never dared to imagine. She shared her story with a few of her newfound friends. Slowly, hesitantly at first, then gaining confidence, she told them everything and was astonished when they cried with her rather than blaming her for the abuse she had endured.

Marcie's trust sense had been damaged. Emboldened by her friends' acceptance, she swung to the opposite extreme of the trust scale and began telling others. Eventually almost every conversation she had included a request such as "Please pray for me today, I'm really struggling with anger at my ex-husband for forcing me to have sex with his best friend while he watched." TMI alert!

Some people did reject Marcie when they first heard her story because they viewed her as damaged by her past and unsalvageable. These people certainly did not understand or offer the grace that God lavished on Marcie. Other friends who wanted to reach out to her found themselves overwhelmed with the information she shared and how much of it she shared. They began to avoid conversations with her so they wouldn't hear any more about her past. In doing so they rejected her, too.

Fortunately for Marcie, a few caring people pointed out the effects of her sharing and guided her in repairing and training her trust sense. She learned that she needed to trust people to be healthy, but that she didn't need to entrust every detail of her life to everybody in order to be totally honest.

Marcie found three people she could trust—a counselor and two close friends who agreed to be prayer partners with her. She told them her story and shared daily struggles and burdens with them. She built mutually supportive (not dependent) relationships with her prayer partners, lifting up their concerns in intercession, too.

She also learned that some people could not handle knowledge of her past. Some couldn't be trusted to keep her confidence. Some judged her and others backed away. Marcie grew in trust and authenticity. She learned that honesty didn't require displaying every aspect of the past and present for the whole world to see; it meant knowing herself and being willing to share herself freely with those who proved themselves worthy of her trust and either wanted or needed to know more about her.

We May Experience True Guilt

Sometimes becoming authentic brings us face to face with our sin and true guilt. God chose David to reign as king. The prophet Samuel called David "a man after [God's] own heart" (1 Sam. 13:14). In spite of all his success, David gave in to the temptations of power, which culminated in his sin with Bathsheba. He became a man far removed from the honest, open shepherd boy who had slain the giant.

It took another prophet, Nathan, to set David on the road to self-discovery and authenticity. Nathan used the story of the rich man with many flocks and the poor man with one sheep because he knew that David was too blind to see himself honestly. For the king, authenticity resulted in recognition of his true guilt.

David provides a wonderful example for us of how to respond: he admitted his sin against God, repented, and asked forgiveness. It is significant that after his initial awareness of his true self, David acknowledged that God desires "truth in the inner parts" of our lives (Ps. 51:6a NIV).

If you experience true guilt on your journey of self-discovery, follow the example of David. Own your guilt; admit it to God. Ask for grace and cleansing. Make Psalm 51 your personal prayer.

We Will Have to Work Hard

I have done a lot of counseling over the years with adults who experienced childhood physical and sexual abuse. Each of these people had decided, for their own unique reasons, that after years of repressing their memories, denying their pain, and trying to pretend it never happened, the time had come to face their past. In my first session with each person, I gave them a guarantee and a warning: "It will get worse before it gets better, but it will never get really better until you go through the 'worst' and do the hard work."

I can give the same guarantee about the process of self-discovery; it will involve hard work. You may unearth painful memories. You will certainly have to acknowledge shortcomings and failures.

You will also find buried treasure! You have gifts and abilities that you haven't allowed yourself to believe existed, and you will discover passions and dreams that you need to nurture. You will recall happy memories that delight and surprise you.

Discovering and embracing both the good and the bad, the pleasing and the displeasing, can take a lot of energy. At times it may seem easier just to close the backstage door on your self and accept the script that someone else is waiting to hand you, complete with mask and foreign persona. After all, you might say, if I live my life someone else's way and it doesn't work out, I can always blame them. I don't have to think for myself, just ask, "What do people expect from me?" and follow blindly. When I walk into a wall or stumble over a curb or get burned-out from playing a role, I can assume the martyr's line, "I was only trying to please them. It's not my fault." If you have trouble identifying your likes and dislikes and your dreams for the future, perhaps you need to consider whether you have accepted someone else's plans for yourself.

That path only *seems* easier. Over the long term, it requires ever-increasing levels of energy and often results in frustration because we cannot be all things to all people. P. T. Barnum is reputed to have said, "You can fool some of the people all of the time, and all of the people some of the time, but you cannot fool all of the people all of the time."

Trying to please everyone becomes ceaseless striving. Investing the effort now in discovering yourself and determining to live authentically throughout your life and ministry will reap rewards in future inner peace.

Kevin* began having panic attacks during his second year of seminary. By the time he came to talk to me he had begun to avoid conversations with other students and found himself spending more and more time alone at home, unable to focus on anything but his distress. Kevin's first panic attack had occurred in preaching class the first day of the term. As he read through the syllabus, the very thought of standing to speak in front of a group of people terrified him. His heart raced and he broke into a cold sweat.

While Kevin recounted this incident to me, his hands shook. He lamented, "Actually, just thinking about being a pastor scares me. If I could just study the Bible all day and write messages, I'd be OK, but I can't imagine myself doing the rest of the job." So I did what made sense to me and asked why he was in seminary if he didn't want to be a pastor. With a deep sigh, he responded, "Because I've been called to ministry and I can't back down now!"

Over several weeks, Kevin and I explored his call. As a high school student, he had been attracted to a girl in his class. He went to church to spend time with her and there he heard the gospel for the first time and became a Christian. In his zeal for his newfound faith, Kevin expressed a desire to serve God, which his girlfriend interpreted as a call to ordained ministry. He announced to his nonbelieving family that he would become a pastor and the die was cast. Kevin had accepted the script that had been handed to him along with his new faith—to become a pastor. With support from his new church friends, Kevin set his sights on Christian college, then seminary.

Now, seven years after he first stated his intention to serve God, Kevin told me that he thought he could serve God well as an active layman and that he would use everything he had learned in college and seminary to be the best Christian husband and church leader possible. He knew his training would not be wasted, but he also knew he could not pastor a church. He had come to know enough about himself to see that he did not have the gifts or the emotional makeup for pastoral ministry.

Once Kevin knew what he did *not* want to do, he had to discover in himself what he *did* want to do. He took several months to investigate career options and further education programs; he underwent personality and gifts assessments with a counselor. Although he had to work hard, his energy level and lack of panic attacks told him this work was focused in the right direction. One of the hardest things for him to do was to tell his family his decision to leave seminary. He feared what they would say about his faith and about God because of this change in his plans.

Kevin applied and was accepted into a doctoral program in another field of work. The university where he went even offered him a teaching fellow position, so he earned a stipend and free tuition for his program. Today, he is working in his chosen field and teaching a Sunday school class in the church were he and his wife attend. He did the hard work of discovering himself and building upon what he discovered. Today, he is reaping the benefits of that work.

Authenticity—What It Is *Not*

I have likened the process of self-discovery to a treasure hunt. In any journey of discovery, we need caveats or warnings to tell us,

"If you reach this point, you've gone too far" or "You missed a turn." In the process of becoming authentic there are several things to avoid.

Authenticity Is Not Selfish

Perhaps the greatest misunderstanding about the process of self-discovery arises out of a belief that such an effort is selfish. As Christians we fear becoming prideful or self-centered. We may have heard sermons urging us to leave our pasts behind and press on toward the future in serving God and serving others. We have learned the acronym that true JOY means "Jesus first, others next, and yourself last."

The appropriate and balanced process of self-examination that leads to and maintains authenticity is not narcissistic navel-gazing. If you begin to think you are the center of the universe, you have missed the intention of this process. Sharing your process of becoming an authentic self with a trusted friend can help alert you to this self-centered thinking if it develops. Self-examination needs to consider strengths, gifts, and weaknesses in a balanced perspective. The ultimate purpose of this process is that, given those advantages and disadvantages, we are able to serve God and others to the best of our ability. The purpose of looking at the past is to learn what we can, in order to resolve any unfinished business, thereby freeing us to more fully engage in the present and the future.

Authenticity Is Not Only Negative

On the other side of the scales, the process of self-examination should not only focus on deficiencies, flaws, and mistakes. If we allow ourselves to wallow in what we cannot do or berate ourselves for our imperfections, we will never believe we have anything to offer to God as living sacrifices, as Paul commanded in Romans

12:1. Self-discovery must also include recognizing strengths and gifts as well as potential for future growth.

The truly authentic person does not open him- or herself indiscriminately for everyone to see. We can learn to be appropriately open and transparent without causing others to run from us shouting, "TMI!" The purpose of looking at our dark side is to set realistic goals, to allow God's strength to work in our weakness, and to become better servants of others and of God in the present and the future.

Authenticity Is Not an Excuse

Some people respond to the self-examination process by saying, "That's just the way I am, and now I have the test report to prove it. I can't change, so love me or leave me." Self-knowledge is not an excuse to quit growing or developing or an excuse for poor behavior. Self-knowledge helps us identify areas of our lives to which we need to give extra attention so that we avoid setting ourselves up to fail.

The role of pastoral ministry is complex. Every pastor, church board, and denominational structure has a long list of expectations and role descriptions for the pastoral leader. No single pastor is a 100 percent match to those expectations. No pastor can do every task of ministry with equal skill and comfort. Becoming truly authentic and self-aware is not an excuse to pick and choose among the list of pastoral expectations only those things that are a good fit and refuse to do those things that are not comfortable. However, the pastor who understands his gifts and strengths can seek opportunities to use those gifts in the best way to the glory of God and the building up of the kingdom. If that same pastor is aware of his weaknesses, he can understand why certain tasks of ministry drain him and arrange his day in ways that compensate for that energy loss. He can also equip others to minister in those areas where he is not strongly gifted. Ministry is enhanced and all the church benefits when the pastor becomes truly authentic.

Assessment Journal

Before you go on to the next chapter, begin an Assessment Journal. This journal is for you, so the format needs to be one that fits you. For some, this journal will be a beautiful, bound blank book. For others it may be a spiral notebook or a three ring binder with loose-leaf paper. You may prefer to write at your computer and keep a journal file. Whatever format you choose to use, I encourage you to find a way to keep it private, so that you can be totally honest with yourself and with God in your writing. To get the most from what you read, maintain this journal consistently throughout the rest of the book.

Thoughtfully answer the following questions before you turn to the next chapter:

1. Draw your own Johari Window. What does it look like—how big is each quadrant? What would you like to change? How will you work to do that?
2. Whom do you trust? Have you identified people in your life that are not safe to trust?
3. Draft a personal response to this popular saying: "What you are is God's gift to you. What you do with it is your gift to God."

2

Self-Assessment

Strengths and Growing Edges

The insurance company that provides our family's health coverage believes in the value of preventive medicine. They will pay (at least in part) for regular physical exams and testing in hopes of minimizing necessary treatment and costs if problems are detected early in their progression. I breathe a sigh of relief when the lab reports come back "within normal limits." The doctor always seems to offer a word or two of advice on my areas of weakness, too: "You need to exercise more" or "Stay away from the sweets." The goal of the checkup is to affirm what is working and to make necessary recommendations for improvement for the purpose of sustaining a longer, healthier life. I usually leave the doctor's office feeling I know a little bit more about my body.

The self-assessment process is like an annual checkup for your whole being. Each of us is given certain strengths, God-given abilities, and potential. We honor God and cooperate with our Creator when we discover these and build on them. We also all have weaknesses and broken places in our lives. We honor God when we honestly confess these places where we need to grow and cooperate with the Spirit in healing and maturing. The goal of the self-assessment process is to affirm what is working and to identify areas of recommended improvement for the purpose of sustaining a longer, healthier life and ministry.

An accurate self-knowledge is balanced. Bookstore and library shelves overflow with guides to self-love, self-affirmation, and the power of human potential and positive thinking. Often Christians react negatively to those (and rightly so) because their humanistic foundations and self-centeredness do not provide a balanced assessment.

We can be truly healthy in our self-awareness if we balance two truths. First, God's word assures us that "there is no one righteous, not even one" (Rom. 3:10; see also Ps. 12:1-3) and we all fall short of the glory of God (Rom. 3:23). Sin separates us from God; our fate is death. The second truth is that we are created in God's image (Gen. 1:27) and called to be children of God the Father. God the Son loved us so much that he gave himself for us "while we were still sinners" (Rom. 5:8) and has entrusted the ministry of God's church to us. God the Spirit gifts and empowers us for that ministry. These two truths require us to balance the knowledge of ourselves as we *would be* but for the grace of God with the knowledge of who we *are and will be* because of the grace of God.

God guides us on the treasure hunt to discover our strengths and weaknesses. King David prayed, "Search me, God, and know my heart; test me and know my anxious thoughts. See if there is any offensive way in me, and lead me in the way everlasting" (Ps. 139:23-24). David sought God's assessment of his emotions (heart), his thoughts, and his behavior (way); he asked for a thorough examination. The apostle Paul also called believers to an accurate self-assessment: "Do not think of yourself more highly than you ought, but rather think of yourself with sober judgment, in accordance with the faith God has distributed to each of you" (Rom. 12:3).

Note: Throughout this chapter, you may think of things you would like to write in your Assessment Journal. I encourage you to read through the whole chapter first to get the big picture before you start writing. Then, using the questions at the end of the chapter as a guide, write in your journal as you launch your own self-discovery process.

I introduced the Johari Window (see Figure 2.1) in the last chapter. The goal of self-assessment is to move the vertical line between "known to self" and "unknown to self" to the right, increasing the areas in which you know yourself. You can minimize the "unknown" quadrant by taking an honest inventory, including, but not limited to, paper and pencil assessments. In the next section, I suggest some tools I have found to be helpful.

	Known to Self	Unknown to Self
Known to Others	Open Pane: known to self and others	Blind Pane: blind to self, seen by others
Unknown to Others	Hidden Pane: open to self, hidden from others	Unknown Pane: unknown to self and others

Figure 2.1. Johari Window

You can also minimize the "blind" quadrant through honest interaction with others. Have you ever wondered what people *really* think of you? We can all benefit from having a few trusted friends in our lives who will speak the truth in love (Eph. 4:15) about both our strengths and our need for improvement. Once you have thoughtfully completed your self-assessment at the end of this chapter, consider whom you might ask to go over each area of possible strengths and weaknesses with you.

One warning is in order: if you do ask someone else to do this, you have to be willing to listen nondefensively and prayerfully consider everything they tell you. Choose this person (or persons) wisely. If your "trust meter" is not working as I described in the last chapter, you might want to delay a while in deciding who to trust, or you might consider asking a professional counselor to work with you on the assessment and on building healthy trust levels.

Strengths

The positive is the best place to begin our assessment. For some Christians, this is the hardest part because we fear appearing prideful. When we consider that "every good and perfect gift is from above, coming down from the Father" (James 1:17), we honor God by acknowledging the gifts God has lavished upon us. We actually insult God when we deny our gifts in the name of modesty. So, let's begin our inventory of strengths.

Physical Resources

Physical resources are easy for us to take for granted, at least until we lose them. So we will consider those first, lest they be neglected. Your first physical resource is yourself—your body, physical strength, and health. We are "fearfully and wonderfully made" (Ps. 139:14). God has called us to serve and has equipped us with the physical capacity to do so. Our service may range from sedentary tasks, such as sermon preparation or reading aloud to a senior adult with failing vision, to participating in physically demanding construction projects either locally or on a foreign mission field.

As you begin enumerating your resources, include your eyesight, hearing, manual dexterity, strength, and overall health. You may discover as a result of your self-assessment that you need to have a physical checkup with your physician. Acknowledging that these physical resources are all gifts from our Creator encourages us to truly value them and do all we can to protect, preserve, and enhance them by caring for our bodies, the temples of the Holy Spirit (1 Cor. 6:19). If you identify physical health and fitness as an area of personal concern, you might benefit from reading *Fit to be a Pastor: A Call to Physical, Mental, and Spiritual Fitness* by Lloyd Rediger. Rediger calls this book a primer on body-mind-spirit fitness.

Financial Resources

Financial resources are another important area to consider. Most of the time when I mention money to pastors or seminary students, the response is something like, "I'll always be poor, because pastors never make enough to live on." Indeed, I have never encouraged anyone to enter ministry to become rich materially. However, you don't have to be wealthy to have financial resources. Let's consider several possibilities. One or more may apply to you.

For some pastors, their greatest financial resource is a profession or skill that helps them earn a living for their family and also serve in a ministry setting that could not otherwise afford to support a pastor. I know of pastors who work part time as attorneys, consultants, substitute teachers, CPAs, and tax preparers. Dean* had worked for more than twenty-five years as a steamfitter before God called him into ministry. He continued in that work while he was in seminary. At graduation, he counted the years until he could retire from construction work and begin collecting his pension. He determined to continue his employment and to volunteer part time in a local church until he qualified for his pension. He recently retired and now serves the church full time as a volunteer.

In other ministry families, the pastor's greatest financial resource is a supportive spouse with a career and income that is sufficient to provide for the family. Many pastors, chaplains, and missionaries are freed to serve in low-paying or volunteer ministries because their spouses believe in their call to serve and are willing to work in order to free them to do so.

We all have financial resources of some kind—possessions, income, financial support from others (for example, from family, social agencies, mission boards). One of the biggest obstacles we face in assessing this area of our resources is our tendency toward a deficit mentality. We find it easier to focus on what we *don't* have than on what we *do* have. We get caught up in comparison with others and with society's standards and find ourselves mired in desire and debt, unable or unwilling to live within our means.

Several excellent resources are available on this topic and several are listed in the bibliography.

Skills and Talents

Skills and talents are things we do well and usually enjoy doing. This category of strengths is one in which our fear of appearing prideful may hinder us greatly. Once we begin noting our strengths, we can always find people with fewer strengths than our own. So we avoid listing our strengths. On the other hand, comparison with others may create a deficit mentality, if we value someone else's abilities above our own and judge ourselves inadequate.

Carrie* is one of the warmest, most accepting people I have ever known. An active lay leader in her church, she is often given tasks where she meets new people, because her pastor recognized her talent for making people feel at ease. One day she dropped by my office and asked to talk. She began crying and kept repeating the phrases "I feel so useless" and "I don't do anything of value" over and over.

Momentarily stunned, I began to remind Carrie of her involvement in various ministries at her church and of specific individuals whose lives she had touched. She brushed all my words away with a "Big deal! That's nothing" and proceeded to tell me all that she couldn't do. She told me how she had called and sent notes to a neighbor who also went to her church and how the other woman did not return her calls and ignored Carrie at church. "Evidently, I can't even be a good friend," she muttered.

Carrie had focused on one "failure" and saw it as evidence of her inadequacy. I challenged her to make a list of all the things she did well, no matter how insignificant they might seem at the moment. She reluctantly said she would try, but she went away defeated, continuing to construct her list of things other people did well that she didn't.

Pastors create comparison lists, too. Many ministers have told me they dread regional conferences or pastors' retreats because these events serve to reinforce in their minds how they don't measure up to their peers.

So, as you assess your skills and talents, I challenge you to silence whatever inner voice reminds you of what you cannot do. For now, we are just going to focus on what you *can* do, with no "buts" allowed. Let's consider three general areas of talent: mental (cognitive), manual (physical), and social (relational).

Mental assets certainly include intelligence and education. Intelligence encompasses more than IQ scores and manifests itself in a variety of ways. Some people have a gift for thinking analytically. They can look at a situation, consider the pros and cons of several courses of action, and follow a linear thought path, "If you do A, then B will happen, then C will come next," to its logical conclusion.

For other people, intelligence shows itself in conceptual thinking. These people, sitting at a conference room table, can look at a long list of concerns on the board and begin to see patterns and themes emerge. They may even go to the board and sketch out a diagram of how the concerns interrelate. They synthesize the work of the rest of the committee, and the whole group experiences an "ah-ha" moment. Are you a conceptual or an analytical thinker?

As a seminary professor, I believe strongly in the value of formal academic training for ministry. I also recognize that a lot of education takes place in a less formal manner. One of the most intelligent women I know got married right out of high school and soon became pregnant, putting an end to her school years. However, she reads voraciously and attends conferences and seminars to continually hone the gifts that God has given her. She recognizes the value of education in many forms.

Manual skills and talents are an asset to ministry in several ways. For example, athletic skill can provide a good way to stay healthy and it can also open doors to relationships with others who share your interest. Michael* loves to run and had been part of the track team in high school and college. When he finished seminary and moved to a small town for his first pastorate, Michael knew he had to find a way to run to keep in shape. He joined a running club and trained for and participated in his first marathon. As he had anticipated, he loves the physical exertion. What has surprised him is the number of runners who have approached him after their running times to talk about concerns in their lives. Some have even visited his church.

What do you do well with your hands? What do you do well with your body? The possibilities are endless. Some examples might be cooking, carpentry, plumbing, sewing, or painting. These talents might be useful in your ministry as well as personally renewing.

Social and relational strengths are essential for pastors because ministry implies people. The second section of this book focuses in greater detail on relationships. At this point, consider your level of emotional intelligence (EI). So far, we have focused on the first domain of EI, which is self-awareness. The other three domains fall under the umbrella of relational skills. The second domain is self-management, which involves such questions as, "How well do you manage your own emotions?" and "How do you handle tough emotional situations?"

The third and fourth domains of EI are social awareness and social/relationship management. How in tune are you with those around you? Are you able to be aware of and sensitive to others without taking responsibility for their problems and painful emotions?

Relationship management would also include social skills. In a group of people, do you make others comfortable? Can you engage in casual conversation or do you frequently experience awkward lapses of silence? Do people sense that you really care about them?

That is Carrie's greatest gift—she really does care about people and they sense it. So when her neighbor didn't respond, it sent her into a tailspin of self-doubt. Fortunately, she didn't give up on loving, and when another neighbor received a frightening medical diagnosis, Carrie went to the hospital to visit. She hugged her friend and they began to talk. The patient asked questions about God, death, and heaven, then thanked her for talking about topics that everyone else was afraid to talk with her about. Later, Carrie told me "I may not have had the most eloquent theological answers, but she was at peace with God when I left her." Her friend was blessed that day, and Carrie's gift was affirmed.

Social skills come more naturally to some people than to others. The family in which you grew up, your personality, and your life experience all shape your level of social skill and comfort. The good news is that this is not an "either you have it or you don't" issue. People skills can be learned and we will consider some ways to develop them in the next chapter on setting goals.

Personality

Personality really is the essence of who you are as a person and shapes the way you approach ministry. Remember John and his mentor, Everett? Everett loved to make pastoral calls. He came alive when he could spend a whole day visiting shut-ins and hospital patients, bringing them communion, prayer, and Scripture. When John accompanied Everett on his rounds, he found that by mid-morning his energy flagged. By noon, John found himself growing impatient with homebound Mrs. Smith's seemingly endless litany of physical complaints and dreading the next visit. He feared that maybe he didn't have enough compassion to be a minister.

John doesn't lack compassion. He lacks self-knowledge. Everett is an extravert. He draws his energy from people, which is why he thrives on a day filled with appointments. John is an introvert. His energy source is the internal world of thoughts and ideas. He is very caring and socially skilled, but no amount of compassion will change the fact that being with people, especially in large groups or for extended time periods, takes energy from him. He

needs to plan his schedule accordingly. As John acquires greater
self-knowledge, his pastoral style will likely include one or two
visits followed by quiet study time for balance and energy.

John *cannot* be Everett, nor should he try to be Everett. John
needs to be himself. He needs to be his *best* self. Personality assessment can help us tap into our strengths and work with them
to maximize our ministry effectiveness.

Some people are wary of personality assessment tools because
they have seen them misused. At a pastor's retreat, I sat down at
a table with seven other people at breakfast time. I greeted the
people I knew and introduced myself to a new pastor and his wife
whom I had never met. No more than five minutes into the table
conversation, this new pastor looked at me and, out of the blue,
said "You're a sanguine;[1] I can tell." He launched into a monologue
on that particular model of understanding personality. I alternated
between feelings of anger and embarrassment.

Personality assessment is *not* a party game or a voyeuristic
pursuit. The final goal of assessment is self-knowledge and growth,
not labeling or putting people in nice, neat, predictable boxes.

One of the best things that my husband, our children, and I
did as a family was to the take the Myers-Briggs Type Indicator
(MBTI) together. I don't think it is an overstatement to say it
transformed relationships personally and professionally for all of
us. The MBTI is a positive tool. It identifies preferences without
a value judgment. The reported type and interpretive material are
descriptive and not prescriptive. In other words, you might read,
"Since your answers indicate you are an extravert, you *may* prefer
large crowds," and you should *never* read "You *must* like technical
manuals because you are a sensate."

A number of good resources are available to explain the
concepts of the MBTI and personality type in great detail.[2] Roy
Oswald and Otto Kroeger wrote a helpful and thorough application of type principles to pastoral ministry.[3] I recommend that

all pastors take this inventory from a certified administrator[4] and prayerfully consider interpretive materials such as those listed in the bibliography.

For purposes of your current self-discovery process, let's consider a brief summary of the four preference scales of the MBTI: Extraversion or Introversion, Sensing or iNtuition, Feeling or Thinking, and Judging or Perceiving.

E/I
This first scale, extraversion (E) or introversion (I), assesses your "preferred world" or energy source. People who indicate a preference for introversion tend to draw their energy from the inner world of thoughts and ideas. They often find that people, especially in large groups, drain them. Extraverts, on the other hand, often are energized by people (the outer world) and find groups innervating. Time alone to ponder can sap energy from the extravert.

S/N
The sensing (S) or intuitive (N) scale measures a person's preferred mode of taking in information. Those who score a high S preference tend to report high use of their five senses— smell, touch, taste, sight, and hearing—to gather data. This usually results in a focus on details, facts, and quantifiable proofs. Alternatively, the person with a high N preference more often uses intuition—a sixth sense—to gather information. This person often notices trends and patterns and envisions complex schemes with minimal focus on the details of a budget or specific steps required to accomplish the vision.

T/F
The third scale assesses what the individual considers most in the process of decision making: thinking (T) or feeling (F). The thinker prefers to apply logic, facts, and standards of right and

wrong when seeking a decision. In contrast, those who indicate a preference for feeling consider personal values, their own
feelings, and the feelings of others in decision making. They might
reject hard-and-fast rules in favor of a case-by-case consideration
because, as they see it, each situation is unique.

J/P

The last scale looks at a person's preference for dealing with the
world. A preference for perceiving (P) suggests the individual likes
to keep taking in information, leaving options open for new input.
Perceivers tend to be spontaneous and flexible. On the other side
of the scale, a preference for judging suggests the individual prefers
to make decisions, to finish projects, and to find closure. Judgers
tend to like things planned, orderly, and organized.

As you read these brief descriptions, you may have thought,
"Well, I do all of those things. How do I know my type?" We all
do all eight of these things on any given day. The key to understanding personality preferences is to ask on each scale which you
do most naturally, most often, or which you prefer. Usually, our
preference is the one we rely on most automatically; therefore, we
have honed our skills in that preference. The other ends of the
scales are those things we choose least often, and we may not do
as well. Using these less-developed abilities is like holding a pen in
your nondominant hand and trying to write your name. You can
do it with great thought and effort, but your first few attempts
may be illegible.

Other valuable tools have been developed that can help us
discover other aspects of our personalities. The Gallup organization
has developed the StrengthsQuest program and has published related resources, including the Clifton StrengthsFinder assessment.[5]
This questionnaire identifies five major themes of talent for each
individual (out of thirty-four possible strength areas) and specifically addresses the implications of those strengths for learning and
career development.

Spiritual Type

Spiritual type is a concept introduced by Urban T. Holmes and further developed by Corinne Ware.[6] In her book, *Discover Your Spiritual Type: A Guide to Individual and Congregational Growth,* Ware developed a model, using what Holmes called the Circle of Sensibility. The circle is formed by two perpendicular lines or axes. The first axis describes ways in which we approach knowing and learning about God; the opposite ends or poles of that axis are affective (heartfelt) and speculative (intellectual). The other intersecting axis asks the question of how one conceptualizes God. The extremes are apophatic (mystery, God as Spirit) and kataphatic (imaging, God as revealed). These two axes form four quadrants, each of which represents a spiritual type that Ware explored. She developed the Spirituality Wheel Selector test, which can be used to determine spiritual type for an individual or a worshiping community. Ware maintains that spiritual type is innate and inner directed. She also argued that spiritual health is related to understanding the importance and contribution of all four elements and to seeking balance while identifying personal and congregational preferences.

Spiritual gifts are given by God to all believers. Scripture provides lists of gifts (Rom. 12:6-8; 1 Cor. 12:4-11; Eph. 4:11-12). Many books have been written and inventories offered. One of the major limitations of such inventories is that they are based on self-reporting, yet spiritual gifts are best discerned in community. The Bible tells us that gifts are given for the building up of the body of Christ, so regardless of what an assessment tool says, we ought to seek confirmation from fellow believers about our gifts. The church functions most efficiently when people know their gifts and function within them.

A cautionary note is in order: knowing your spiritual gifts is not an excuse to avoid those aspects of your pastoral role for which you are not particularly gifted. For example, some believers have a spiritual gift of evangelism, but all believers are called to share the good news. Some pastors simply state, "It's not in my gift mix" and ignore significant portions of their job descriptions, much to the dismay of their congregations.

Passion

Passion is the fuel that energizes the use of our other strengths. Passion is what motivates you and gets you out of bed in the morning. Passion will keep a pastor going in the midst of conflict or discouragement. Your passion may be an area of interest or an activity in which you love to participate. This interest area may be an asset in ministry, providing an open door to meet people.

Growing Edges

Part of an honest self-assessment is recognizing places in our lives that are not strengths. The opposite of strength is weakness, so I will use that word, but I prefer to think of weaknesses as growing edges—those places where I need to grow, the rough edges of my life. We all have them and it is better to face them rather than to hope they will just go away if we ignore them.

Paul wrote to the Corinthians, "We have this treasure in jars of clay to show that this all-surpassing power is from God and not from us" (2 Cor. 4:7). Our limitations actually show that our power comes from God; God is glorified when we acknowledge them and we don't try to pretend we are perfect.

Parker Palmer wrote of the importance of looking at one's imperfections: "Leadership is hard work for which one is regularly criticized and rarely rewarded, so it is understandable that we need to bolster ourselves with positive thoughts. But by failing to look at our shadows, we feed a dangerous delusion that leaders too often indulge: that our efforts are always well intended, our power is always benign, and the problem is always in those difficult people whom we are trying to lead!"[7]

An honest and healthy reflection on our growing edges focuses on identifying areas for needed and potential growth, not on shaming for times of failure. Shaming only leads to defensiveness and guilt, so it has no place in the assessment process.

Ask Yourself

Personal reflection is the first step in identifying our weaknesses. Spend some time searching your mind regarding the questions listed in the Assessment Journal section at the end of this chapter.

Ask Others

Input from others can help in discovering our growing edges. Often personal weaknesses fall in the "blind" quadrant of the Johari window—others can see them, but we cannot. You can benefit when you are honest and vulnerable enough to ask for feedback from people you trust to have your best interests in mind.

Often in the course of identifying blind spots, we encounter unresolved, open emotional wounds. When we do find them, we must face them head-on and find healing so they don't hinder relationships in the future. Many otherwise successful pastoral ministries have been destroyed by unresolved emotional pain in the pastor's past that eventually caught up with her.

Use the Myers-Briggs Type Indicator

The MBTI can help you identify growing edges. Each of the preferences has a potential downside or negative effect from the extreme dependence on or misuse of that preference. For example, the extravert may spend so much time with other people, drawing energy from social interaction, that she neglects her inner world and becomes shallow and superficial. The perceiver may take flexibility and spontaneity to the extreme and frustrate others with procrastination and laziness.

The preferences themselves are neither good nor bad, but just tendencies. A healthy way to use personality assessment is to seek to maximize the strengths of our preferences and avoid the extremes and pitfalls.

In the process of using the assessment tools referred to and answering the questions raised in this chapter, you may have identified areas of concern in your life for which you would be wise to seek professional help. This help may come from a professional counselor, a life coach, or a spiritual director. Whatever time and money you may spend on this process will be an investment in your overall well-being and the future of your ministry.

Some weaknesses are deficits, which makes them truly growing edges. Something is lacking in your life, which holds you back, limiting your effectiveness and perhaps your life satisfaction. Perhaps in the assessment process, you will identify an area of your life in which you need to add on or increase to reduce the existing deficit. Maybe you need to increase your patience, learn a new skill, or improve your physical self-care. You may identify that you need to build your emotional intelligence. The good news is that you can do any of these things if you are willing to set goals and work on your growth.

Some weaknesses are *not* deficits; at least they are not places where you have a lot of potential for growth or for change. Sometimes our weaknesses are simple reality, such as age and physical limitations. These weaknesses need not keep us from ministry, but we must accept them and learn to work within the limits they impose upon us. One pastor I know has had many years of effective ministry in spite of a diagnosis of rheumatoid arthritis and his doctor's orders that he nap every day. He and his congregations learned to live with and respect this physical restriction.

The Assessment Journal section provides a structured outline and questions for the self-discovery process. These questions are really only the beginning of what will be a lifelong process of discovering the richness with which God has created you. May this truly become a treasure hunt for you.

Assessment Journal

The following outline presents questions in each area of strengths and growing edges. Respond to each question as thoroughly as possible to create a comprehensive self-assessment. Take as much time as you need to do this thoroughly; your self-assessment will become the foundation of your Personal and Professional Growth Plan.

1. Physical Resources
   - How is your general health?
   - What do you do to maintain good physical condition?
2. Financial Resources
   - List *all* of the financial resources you can think of that are available to you: your own profession or skill that might provide additional income, your spouse's career skills, possessions, outside funding sources (grants, mission agencies).
   - What is your current debt load?
   - What spending habits have you developed?
   - Are your spending habits a strength or a weakness?
3. Mental Assets
   - List your educational strengths. Begin with your degrees and diplomas, whatever they may be. Then consider the following questions to identify assets:
   - Are you a conceptual or an analytical thinker?
   - What are you reading?

- What continuing education courses have you taken?
- What seminars or conferences have you attended?
- Do you belong to a Bible study group or book club?

4. Manual Skills or Talents
   - What do you do well with your hands?
   - What do you do well with your body? Make a list. Some examples might be cooking, carpentry, plumbing, sewing, or painting.
   - As you look at your list, which two or three of these talents are the most essential in your life? How are they energizing or renewing for you? How might these talents be useful in your ministry?

5. Social or Relational Strengths
   - How well do you manage your own emotions?
   - How do you handle tough emotional situations? Do you fly off the handle easily? Do you keep things bottled up inside until you explode? Do you isolate yourself from others to avoid dealing with painful emotions? Or are you able to acknowledge your feelings and control your response to them?
   - How in tune are you with those around you? Are you able to be aware of and sensitive to others without taking responsibility for their problems and painful emotions?
   - How would you rate your social skills? In a group of people, do you make others comfortable? Can you engage in casual conversation or do you frequently experience awkward lapses of silence? Do people sense that you really care about them?

6. Personality
   - Indicate your preference on each of the four Myers-Briggs scales described in the chapter (E or I, S or N, T or F, J or P). If you have taken the MBTI recently, indicate your preference letters and scores in your

journal. If you haven't taken the inventory, use the descriptions in this chapter to help you estimate your preferences.

- What do you see as the greatest benefits or strengths of your preferences on these scales? For example: "I'm an introvert and I really enjoy time alone for study and sermon preparation."

7. Spiritual Gifts
   - List what you consider to be your spiritual gifts.
   - What gifts have others identified in you?
   - If you have taken any spiritual gift inventories, what were the results?
   - What evidence do you see in your life and ministry of the gifts that you have listed?

8. Passion
   - What are you passionate about?
   - To help you identify passion, think of a time when you did something and felt great while you were doing it, just enjoying the doing of it.
   - What would you do if there were no constraints—if time, money, and pleasing other people were no object?
   - If you were to die today, what would be one thing you would regret not doing?

9. Growing Edges
   - What don't you do well?
   - What do you avoid doing? Why?
   - What have you always wished you could do but never learned how?
   - Identify any areas of your MBTI preference that may currently be or become weaknesses for you. How might you strengthen the opposite side of that preference scale to grow personally?

3

Setting Your Direction

When my husband Keith and I travel somewhere new, we have developed a system that has grown out of using our strengths. He is the organizer and planner. I am more spontaneous and last minute in my day-to-day life. Usually, before our trip, we talk about what we would like to do and see along the way and at our destination. Keith calculates distances, estimates travel time, and makes whatever reservations are necessary: airplane tickets, car rental, hotel or motel rooms, and so forth. Wherever we are, once in the car, Keith drives and I navigate. You will find me in the passenger's seat with the map open on my lap, mentally crossing off street names as we pass them and pointing out landmarks.

The process of assessing strengths and weaknesses is like drawing a personal map. Maps help us identify where we are and keep us from getting lost. But, by themselves, maps don't get us anywhere. We have to decide on a final destination and map out the route and itinerary to get there. In our lives and our ministries, goals establish our intended destination and plans provide a travel itinerary, helping us decide the best way to get to our goals and identify our progress along the way. Without goals and plans, we might wander aimlessly through life and reach the end of the trip frustrated or disappointed with our final destination.

One time, and *only* one time, we decided to wing it. I was in charge and we would do vacation my laid-back, spontaneous way. We opted to take a weekend trip without a travel plan. We did call ahead and make reservations for Friday night in a motel on the beach in southern Washington State. Our only final goal was to be home in Portland, Oregon, by Sunday night.

We enjoyed our first night in Long Beach, exploring the coastal town and walking barefoot in the sand. With no alarm clock the next day, we had a leisurely morning and climbed in the car to begin our adventure. I had a vague notion that we would drive north on Highway 101 through the Olympic peninsula and end up in Port Angeles for the night, then work our way back down south on the other side of the peninsula the next day. We drove and talked—conversations we hadn't taken time for in months. We enjoyed each other's company as we passed through miles of evergreen forests.

As we approached the largest hotel in Port Angeles, I had the first warning of trouble. I read the sign over the entrance: WEL-COME, LITTLE LEAGUE BASEBALL TOURNAMENT. The place was full. As a matter of fact, the clerk assured me, every place in town was full.

No problem. We would just go on down the road to the next town. According to the map, that was Sequim. When we reached Sequim, we had no success finding a room. Still, no problem. We decided to try Port Townsend. I had always wondered what Port Townsend looked like but had never been there. We drove through the main street in heavy traffic. This looked like a great place for a vacation. People crowded the sidewalks, going in and out of restaurants along the way. "No vacancy" messages shone from every motel and hotel sign in sight. The same was true all along Highway 101 as we made our way south on the other side of the Olympic Peninsula loop.

After ten hours in the car, looking at scenery and talking, we ended up in Olympia, just one hour from where we had started that morning and just two hours from home!

Fortunately, Keith is a patient man. We really *had* needed the time alone together to talk, which the long drive amply provided. And we had friends in Olympia whom we called, and we went to breakfast and church with them the next day. But we missed out on all the little towns and turnouts I had hoped to explore because we had to focus instead on looking for a place to sleep.

I learned that a little bit more planning would have actually made our "free" time even more enjoyable, freeing us to be more flexible along the way. I never asked for a trip done "my way" again. Ever since that weekend, our shared travel system has resulted in better trips for both of us.

Goals and Plans

Life is a long journey. All pastors, and probably most adults, can benefit from taking the time to identify and write down long-term and short-term goals for their lives and ministries.

The work that you have done in the previous chapters in getting to know yourself better is the first step. You have surveyed the terrain and now it is time to draw your map. This chapter focuses on helping you to develop goals and plans to meet those goals. You will develop a Personal and Professional Growth Plan that will serve as your travel itinerary. Think of goals as your intended destination and of plans as your route and means of transportation on the journey.

Setting Goals

One way to make a growth plan is to think in terms of categories, an approach which lends to creating a chart. The chart might have the following headings: personal (with subheadings for physical and relational), professional, spiritual, and intellectual/mental. The next step would be to list goals under each column.

For some people this method may work well; the organized, methodical approach will provide clear direction. In doing this, you may find that certain goals fit under two or more categories. Where do you put them? You end up with a lot of overlap and arrows drawn between columns to show connections. Just as we are all complex, multifaceted persons, our goals will be multifaceted and interrelated. If you are frustrated by the overlap when focusing on categories, try thinking of goals in terms of time instead. Focus on setting long-term (five to ten years or more) and short-term (one to three years) goals.

In this chapter, you will find examples of a wide range of areas in which you might identify goals. At the end of the chapter is a series of questions to answer in your Assessment Journal that will guide you in the process of establishing goals. In every area you will be asked to write out short-term and long-term goals. For every long-term goal, identify one or more short-term goals ("pit stops" on the journey) as an indicator of progress toward the larger goal.

For example, let's say that you believe God has called you to spend your life in Africa ministering to families affected by HIV/AIDS. Within the next seven years, you want to be living in Africa full time. Short-term goals might include paying off all debts within the next three years, contacting existing mission agencies, researching HIV/AIDS ministries worldwide, and in the next four years learning an African dialect for the region in which you intend to minister.

Focusing on Strengths and Assets

Often when we think about goal setting, our focus immediately turns to our shortcomings and how we might correct them. How often do you hear people express New Year's resolutions to lose weight or to become more organized or to break a certain bad habit? None of those are bad intentions, but because the focus is

on eliminating a negative, motivation lags quickly and discouragement sets in.

Pastors too often try to set goals before they do the hard work
of self-discovery. They may end up with a one-size-fits-all plan with
commendable goals in which they have little investment. The goals
are set with someone else in mind—an image of what a pastor
"should" do. These goals usually fade away for lack of motivation.
On the other hand, goals that are developed for yourself, not for
anyone else's sake, and in conjunction with the road map of your
life will take you a long way in life.

For the best results when you set goals for your life, focus on
developing and building on the foundation of existing strengths
and assets. This principle is true for organizational planning as
well as for individuals.[1] Approaching goal setting with a positive
focus also includes adding on—perhaps new things you have put
off doing or never allowed yourself to imagine were possible.

First Things First: Vision for the Journey—a Case Study

First, we need a vision to inform our goals. The following questions help identify a vision: If you could do anything you dreamed,
if there were no limits or restrictions over the next ten years of
your life . . .

- What kind of person would you like to be? (*to be*)
- What tasks would you like to accomplish? (*to do*)
- What would you like to know? (*to learn*)
- What would you like to be able to do? (skills or patterns
  to develop)

Using these questions as a guide, let's consider the vision and
goals of David, a recent seminary graduate. Note: Later, you will
write your own answers to these questions in your journal. Once
you have a vision for what the future might look like, you can

decide which of these things on your list are most important and begin the process of setting short-term and long-term goals for those that you want to work toward.

David's vision is for long-term pastoral ministry in an urban or suburban setting. He loves to preach and has received affirmation of his gifts in communicating God's word. As an introvert, David finds it easy to take time for study and sermon preparation. He cares deeply about people but has not had a lot of experience in providing pastoral care. He worries a bit that the people demands of ministry will tire him. David and his wife, Sarah, will move in two weeks as he assumes his first pastoral position. They eagerly anticipate the birth of their first child six months from now. David answered the four questions about his vision for the next ten years. This is what he wrote:

To Be

I would like to be known as a faithful pastor who lovingly guides the people of my congregation to deeper levels of faith through my teaching, preaching, and caring ministry. I want to be spiritually vibrant and growing in my faith. I desire to be a great husband and father. I expect to be a lifelong learner.

To Do

I want to visit at least two new countries in the next ten years. I would like to challenge my church to become involved in mission projects both at home and overseas. I want to stay involved in scholarly pursuits to challenge my mind and keep my thinking fresh.

To Learn

I'm excited about becoming a father, but since I haven't spent a lot of time around children, I would like to learn more about child development (what to expect) and parenting. Now that I've finished my seminary program, I have a long list of must-read books. I would like to learn a hobby—something that will allow me to escape from the pressures of life and provide solitude and refreshment to nourish my introvert side. I also would like to learn a second language, which should facilitate the traveling I hope to do.

To Develop

To continue to grow in my faith, I need to develop more consistent spiritual formation practices. I need to continue the good financial management patterns I have begun. In ten years, I want to be financially stable enough to go on both vacation trips and mission project trips. I want to develop my pastoral skills, especially in the area of listening skills and hospital visitation. I want to maintain a physically healthy lifestyle with good diet and adequate exercise.

The Next Step: The Itinerary

Once we have a general direction for the future, we can focus more specifically on establishing targets. Now that we can sense David's vision, let's look at his specific short-term (s) and long-term (l) goals.

To Be

Pastor and Preacher
- Develop a pattern of sermon and worship planning three months at a time (s)
- Read a book on narrative preaching (s)
- Take one course in preaching every two to three years (l)

Husband
- Establish weekly date night with Sarah (s)
- Attend marriage seminar together (l)
- Plan a tenth anniversary trip together without children (l)

Father

- Establish weekly one-on-one times with children (s)
- Read one book on parenting with Sarah every six months (note: this goal will also strengthen their marriage as they communicate about how to raise their children) (s)
- Take children with me, as appropriate, when visiting parishioners (s, l)

Spiritual Growth

- Take annual spiritual retreat (s, l)
- Try new spiritual formation practices and prayer patterns (s)
- Read Bible devotionally every day (s, l)

To Do

- Choose countries to visit (s)
- Develop a study plan—one course each year (s)
- Earn a Doctor of Ministry (DMin) degree (l)
- Take one mission trip with church in the next three years (s)
- Develop a pattern of at least one mission trip every two years (l)

To Learn

- Find a hobby (Web site development, photography, and woodworking are possibilities) (l)
- Take childbirth preparation class with Sarah (s)
- Read parenting books with Sarah (s)
- Learn conversational Spanish (s, l)

To Develop

- Maintain my current weight (s, l)
- Develop exercise routine (in new location, given change in schedule after seminary graduation) (s)
- Review budget, spending, and income (s)
- With Sarah, establish a financial strategy for the present and the future (s, l)

Plans: The Means of Transportation

The next step in setting a personal and professional direction is to determine plans to achieve one's goals. Plans add action steps and a timetable to the goals we establish. As you do this, you may want to seek wise counsel to help you devise a plan.

The story of Moses and his father-in-law Jethro provides an example of planning (Ex. 18:13-27). Jethro was dismayed when he discovered how Moses spent his day—resolving conflicts among the people from dawn until dark. He could see that this exhausted his son-in-law and distracted him from his true calling to teach the people and to represent them to God. Jethro didn't just suggest a goal and say "Rest," but he devised a plan using Moses's strengths (delegation skills) and his assets (qualified leaders). The detailed plan called for officials to serve as judges "over thousands, hundreds, fifties and tens" (v. 21).

David's Timetable and Action Steps

Here are detailed plans that David might establish to reach his vision and goals.

To Be

- Schedule one day every three months for prayer and sermon and worship planning.
- Choose a narrative preaching book and begin reading.
- Contact colleges or seminaries to request a schedule of future preaching courses.
- Schedule (and write on my calendar) date nights with Sarah.
- Explore local options for marriage seminars—get my name on mailing lists for information and announcements.
- On our first date night, dream together about our tenth anniversary trip.

- Begin a file or notebook on our dream destination—for ongoing research.
- Schedule a three-day spiritual retreat for this year.
- Make reservations at a retreat center.
- Choose one new prayer pattern for this month (check my notes from the Spiritual Formation course I took).
- With Sarah, decide on best time to designate for weekly sabbath practice.
- Begin a sabbatical file; investigate denominational policy on clergy sabbaticals.

To Do

- Start a file for each country I want to visit—explore on the Web, or at the library.
- Check the course schedule of nearby schools for continuing education opportunities.
- Research DMin programs online.
- Contact denominational leaders about mission trip opportunities (location, cost, requirements, and so forth).
- Appoint a church Dream Team to explore mission trip possibilities.

To Learn

- Contact the hospital in the new community about childbirth classes.
- Explore options for language and hobby classes—local community college, hobby stores, builders' supply stores, county recreation departments. Collect course schedules.
- Ask Sarah to choose a parenting book we can read together. Start reading.

To Develop

- Walk daily.

- Once we are in the new church, find a place to play basketball at least once a week.
- Now that I have a pastoral position, work with Sarah to establish a new budget.
- Establish a savings and investment plan for our future goals.

Notice that each plan listed is a specific action that flows directly out of one of the goals. A specific target time can be assigned to each plan—"this week," "by June 15," or "next month."

Good Plans: Enhancing Your Chances of Success

The way in which we frame our plans has a lot to do with our success in meeting our goals. Plans that are quantifiable, positive, workable, flexible, expandable, and realistic yet challenging increase the likelihood of achievement. Let's consider David's plans in light of these characteristics.

Quantifiable
When plans are measurable, we can assess progress. David can look at his calendar and count the number of date nights he has scheduled or the frequency of his sermon and worship planning days.

Positive
Too often, we phrase plans in terms of what we will *stop doing*—for example, to consume less sugar or to stop smoking. David's plans all involve what he *will do*.

Workable
If our plans harness the energy of our passion, they will draw us in. Plans provide the "how to" and guidelines to direct the passion toward fulfilling the ultimate goals. David expressed a passion to be a great husband and father. This passion will motivate him to invest

in his marriage through time spent with Sarah, reading together, and attending a marriage retreat in order to reach his goal.

Flexible

Even the most organized, detailed plans need to allow some flexibility. In our journey through life, we will see new signs along the way. Unexpected opportunities may arise and flexible plans allow us to take advantage of them. Crises occur and flexible plans enable us to respond and cope with them. Most of David's plans are implicitly flexible. His plan to decide with Sarah on a time for weekly sabbath practice is an example. At this time in their lives, a weekday may be best for them to set aside sabbath time. As their child grows and begins school, Saturday may become the most obvious time for a family sabbath.

Expandable

As we grow and learn and experience new things, we will be challenged to add more goals to our lists. Plans are not intended to limit us but to provide a structure in which we can move forward and grow.

Realistic yet Challenging

When it comes to challenge, a delicate balance exists between too much and not enough. If our plans seem too lofty and demanding, we may give up in early defeat. However, if we set our sites too low, we may experience boredom and find it easy to procrastinate. David would do well to review his goals and plans regularly and ask himself how well they engage him.

Preparation for the Journey: A Solid Foundation

In previous chapters, we have looked at the importance of knowing ourselves, both strengths and growing edges. I have encouraged you to become truly authentic, to live into your self-awareness and be the best you possible. Your self-assessment allows you to shape your own unique vision, goal, and plans for the journey to which God has called you.

One important caveat remains for us to consider. Some people conclude their self-assessment with a negative perspective. They decide they cannot measure up or that God can't use them because of their inadequacies. No matter where you travel in life, one thing remains consistent—you take yourself along for the journey. All of your goals and planning will have little effect if you don't feel comfortable with who you are. Your thought life can actually sabotage all your good intentions.

In his book *Shame and Grace*, Lewis Smedes differentiates between shame and guilt.[2] We experience guilt over what we do, such as "I feel guilty because I told a lie." We experience shame over who we are, such as, "I feel shame because I am a liar." An accumulation of shameful messages results in a certainty that we do not measure up and probably never will.

People who carry shame find it hard, if not impossible, to develop a Personal and Professional Growth Plan. They don't feel worthy to be where their goals might take them and can't imagine actually meeting whatever goals they might establish.

Smedes emphasizes the healing power of God's grace to overcome shame. He points out that we are all created in God's image and called as God's children to receive grace.

Addressing this healing process in more detail is beyond the scope of this book. If you find yourself struggling with shame, unable to accept grace for yourself, and thus unable to envision and plan for the future, please seek the resources to find healing.[3]

I would suggest three guidelines for you to consider in your relationship with yourself. These things can help you to like yourself, to love the person in your mirror.

Accept Yourself

A colleague once challenged me to be "satisfied with a dissatisfied satisfaction." I like the sound of that! If you have followed the steps in previous chapters, you have done a thorough self-assessment. To accept yourself means balancing "I am comfortable with who I am today" with "There's always room for growth and improvement."

Affirm Yourself

On my desk, I have a *Calvin and Hobbes* comic cut from the newspaper years ago. The young boy, Calvin, stands in front of a mirror in his underwear, flexing his arms in a weightlifter's pose. He says, "Yessir, made in God's image." Over Hobbes's head, the thought bubble reads, "God must have quite a sense of humor."

Affirmation is not merely gazing in a mirror wishfully reciting positive statements. To affirm yourself means to acknowledge the goodness of God's creation, to recognize God's gifts within you. Affirming also includes claiming the truth of Paul's assurance that God "who began a good work in you will carry it on to completion until the day of Christ Jesus" (Phil. 1:6).

Assert Yourself

Secure in your calling as God's child, recognize the validity of your thoughts and feelings. While you listen to and value the thoughts and feelings of others, you also expect that they will hear and value yours. This honest, assertive exchange provides a good foundation for relationships built on grace. As you practice giving grace to yourself, it becomes easier to extend grace to others.

Companions on the Journey

With the secure foundation of self-understanding and acceptance, we can more freely travel the path to which God directs us. The Personal and Professional Growth Plan provides the direction of a map and an itinerary for the journey. We cannot travel this road alone. However noble our goals, we really need others to walk with us and encourage us along the way. In the following chapters, we will explore how to build relationships with God and with other people who join us for the journey.

Assessment Journal

Now that you have seen David's plans, use your Assessment Journal to develop your own Personal and Professional Growth Plan. I believe you may find it very helpful to share your vision, goals, and plans with someone you trust. Ask this person to help you evaluate your plans according to the characteristics listed above. Someone who knows you well can help you assess how realistic your plans are and provide accountability and prayer support for you in working toward your goals.

Vision

Pray and ask God to guide your thoughts as you reflect on the following four questions. If you could do anything you dreamed, if there were no limits or restrictions over the next ten years of your life . . .

- What kind of person would you like to be? (*to be*)
- What tasks would you like to accomplish? (*to do*)
- What would you like to know? (*to learn*)
- What would you like to be able to do? (skills or patterns *to develop*)

Goals

You have done the self-discovery work if you have kept an Assessment Journal through the previous chapters. Before you begin listing goals, take some time to review your journal and what you have identified as your strengths. Consider each of the strengths areas, such as resources, personality, and spiritual gifts, addressed in chapter 2.

- How do you currently use your strengths in ministry?
- Try to envision how you might begin to use strengths that you have recently identified.
- How can you enhance or refine your gifts and use them more fully for personal growth and service to God?

Develop short-term and long-term goals in each area of the vision you have identified—to be, to do, to learn, and to develop.

Plans

Establish specific, detailed plans for each of the goals you have set. Provide a timeline or target date for each. Review your plans to be sure that they are quantifiable, positive, workable, flexible, expandable, and realistic.

Work Your Plan

You have now developed your own personalized Personal and Professional Growth Plan. You can do one of two things. You might put it away in a file and forget about it, perhaps even feel guilty about it every once in a while. Or you can put your plans into action. Keep your Growth Plan where you will see it, and review it often. Allow your vision to guide you in your daily decisions as you seek to become the person that God has created and gifted you to be.

4

Created for Relationship

At the seminary, faculty and students talk a lot about community. Sometimes we just mourn all of the things that hinder a sense of community: our block course schedule, students' full-time jobs, time pressures, and so on. Other times we optimistically brainstorm ways to build community—small group times, chapels, spiritual formation groups—around our adult obstacles. (I have even offered donuts before class if students would come thirty minutes early and just talk to each other!) What we never debate, however, is whether we *need* community. We have assumed that as a given.

Perhaps our certainty stems from our own perceived needs for connection. I know that we need community, because every term I encounter at least two or three students like Andrea* who came by my office and asked tentatively, "Have you got a minute?" I invited her in and, without warning, tears welled up in Andrea's eyes. She said, "I'm so lonely." She rushed on, "I'm thinking about dropping out and moving back somewhere near my folks. This just isn't working out, and I don't know if I can do it any longer!"

Andrea had graduated that spring from a small college and come over 1,500 miles away from her family, her boyfriend, and her home church to attend seminary. With a new roommate, new job, and full course load, she had little time for a social life. She hadn't yet found a church she wanted to attend. Loneliness and isolation overwhelmed her. She needed community—a meaningful connection with others.

Made for Relationship

Loneliness brings pain to our individual lives and to society because it goes against our very nature. God created us for relationship. God said, "It is not good for the man to be alone. I will make a helper suitable for him" (Gen. 2:18). The give and take of relationships is like inhaling and exhaling; we need both to survive. From the moment of conception the child is oriented toward the mother, and at the moment of birth the child depends totally on relationship with others for sustenance.

Our hunger for relationship makes sense when we consider our Creator. The God who designed humankind for relationship is also *in* relationship—God the Father/Creator, Son/Redeemer, and Holy Spirit/Comforter. We find signs of the Trinity in God's words at creation: "Let *us* make human beings in *our* image, in *our* likeness" (Gen. 1:26a, emphasis added). Stephen Seamands, professor of Christian doctrine at Asbury Theological Seminary, maintained that the Trinity "reveals that persons are *essentially* relational."[1]

Good Relationships Foster Good Health

Good relationships build emotional and mental health. Connections with others provide social support, which includes "emotional support (expressions of love, empathy, concern), esteem support (respect for the person's qualities, belief in the person's abilities, validation of the person's thoughts, feelings, or actions), information support (factual input, advice, appraisal of the situation), and tangible assistance (assistance with tasks or physical resources, such as money or a place to live)."[2] Relationships are restorative and nurturing. Robert Putnam, author of *Bowling Alone: The Collapse and Revival of American Community*, states that research shows "Social isolation has many well-documented side effects. Kids fail to thrive. Crime rises. Politics coarsens. Generosity shrivels. Death comes sooner (social isolation is as big a risk factor for premature death as smoking). Well-connected people live longer, happier lives."[3]

Good Relationships Allow Us to Play

Relationships provide a mechanism for refreshment, an outlet that can renew our spirits. Experts in the field of disaster and trauma response know the healing power of humor and play. I recently traveled to New Orleans with a group of seminary students to provide pastoral care for a group of people who had experienced the devastation of Hurricane Katrina. After days of listening to harrowing stories of evacuations, rescues, destruction, and death, our group found refreshment in playing games with the four-year-old son of one of the staff members at the shelter.

In ministry, parishioners invite us into the hidden places of their lives. In daily interactions and especially in times of crisis, we often see people at their worst. The privilege of relaxing and laughing with friends provides a nurturing oasis that will sustain us and remind us of the good in the world.

Your Unique Relationship Style

God created us for relationship. God also created each of us uniquely, so it follows that we each have unique relationship needs. The strength of your preference for extraversion or introversion greatly influences your personal relationship style in several ways.

Extraverts find their energy in the world of people and things. They may thrive on having many friends and acquaintances; some might say that an extravert never meets a stranger. Because of this relationship style, extraverts often seek out social experiences and large-group gatherings, and they enjoy participating in group sports or entertainment experiences for their playtime.

Introverts, on the other hand, find energy in the world of thoughts and ideas. They may prefer one or two deep friendships and perceive the extravert's numerous relationships as shallow. Introverts tend to seek out one-on-one or small-group social interactions, and find greater joy in individual sports or games. Their preference for a smaller social group may limit the number of potential confidants available to the introvert, resulting in a higher risk for loneliness.

Another way that extraversion or introversion preferences affect us relationally is in the way that we process information. If you are an extravert, you probably process your thought externally—out loud. I often hear extraverts say, "I'm not sure what I think until I hear myself say it." External processing, at its best, requires listeners or confidants. Extraverted pastors who allow the stresses of ministry to isolate them may talk to lots of people every day about others' needs, yet may feel starved for someone to talk with about their own personal matters.

By contrast, introverts may "live in their heads," processing their thoughts internally. In times of stress, amidst the demands of ministry, the introverted pastor may retreat into the inner world and become cut off from the support and interpersonal contact that will prevent loneliness.

We all need others, albeit in different ways and to different degrees. In reality, we need balance. We all live in both the world of people and the world of thoughts and ideas. We each simply prefer and draw energy from one world over the other. Understanding your own preference can help you identify your relational style and find appropriate ways to fill your need for social support.

If you are an extravert, you may choose to seek out friends who will help you think things through, people who will listen to you, ask good questions, and help shape your externalized thought processes. If you are an introvert, you might seek out friends who will listen as you tell them what you *have already* thought through and allow you to test out your conclusions with them.

Roles and Relationships

Every relationship implies at least one role and every role implies at least one relationship. Sometimes one role implies many relationships. For example, my relationship with Keith implies the role of wife and also the role of coworker because we work at the same seminary. My role as wife implies only one relationship—with Keith. But my role as coworker implies relationships with a number of colleagues.

Each of us occupies multiple roles in life. I am a wife, mother, sister, sister-in-law, grandmother, friend, professor, committee member on multiple committees, church member, neighbor, and registered voter. I might also list minor roles such as grocery store customer and occasional roles such as Christmas program director. Just writing this list makes me tired! Your list of roles might be even longer than mine.

Each role carries with it expectations. These expectations come from ourselves as well as from others. Some expectations are spoken. Some are written, such as in employment settings where role expectations take the form of a job description and contract.

Unspoken role expectations sometimes become emotional minefields with one person accusing another: "Everyone *knows* that a pastor should call on church visitors within two days!" or "If you were a good father, you would have volunteered to coach the kids' soccer team."

A young woman in a new job met with her supervisor for her three-month performance evaluation. He expressed his overall satisfaction with her work, but also voiced disappointment that she had neglected two tasks which should have been done daily.

She stared in amazement. No one had ever told her those tasks were part of her job! She quickly added them to her daily routine and asked for clarification of other expectations of her in this new role.

If you allow them to, the many roles in your life and the expectations that accompany them can create difficulty and lead to burnout.

Role Conflict

Role conflict comes in several forms. One of the most prevalent develops when two or more people disagree on what the role should look like.

Jeremy* had begun to feel comfortable in his role as pastor at First Community Church. After only six months he felt like he was settling in and finding his pace. One Sunday morning Steve Thompson stopped him in the foyer. "Pastor, I went to the nursing home this week to see Mrs. Reeves. She said she hasn't seen you in three months. You need to give more attention to our shut-ins."

On Monday Pastor Jeremy made a list and set up a visitation schedule so that he could meet Steve's expectations. He made five nursing home calls that week. The next Sunday following the worship service, he looked forward to reporting to Steve how much he had enjoyed his visitation. Before he could find Steve, however, Jeremy ran into Sarah Johnson who said, "I've been trying to reach you all week. Aren't you *ever* in the office? We need a pastor who is accessible!"

Steve and Sarah had competing expectations of what Jeremy should accomplish in his role as pastor. And neither of them even thought to ask Jeremy what he expected of himself in that role. Often pastors run themselves ragged trying to keep everyone happy.

No single individual can meet all of the competing expectations of any role.

Certainly, the role of pastor involves numerous expectations. You have your own mental list of what a good pastor should do. Each person in your congregation also has a list. Even people who don't go to your church, or to any other church for that matter, have expectations of what you will do if you are a good pastor. A significant portion of ministry stress arises due to conflict or uncertainty about those role expectations.

Role conflict also arises when two roles compete for time and attention. Many pastors feel trapped in the tug-of-war between expectations in their clergy role and in their role of spouse and parent. The tension appears at specific times, such as when parent-teacher conferences at the children's school are scheduled on the same night as midweek Bible study. The conflict can also be pervasive, such as the phone ringing nearly every night in the middle of family dinnertime.

Countless pastors like Jeremy flounder in a sea of conflicting and often unspoken expectations. Many clergy families slowly suffocate and break apart after years of losing in the competition for their pastor-spouse's or pastor-parent's time and attention. The unique and often heavy demands of ministry make pastors highly vulnerable to loneliness. A number of pastors unconsciously back away from voluntary relationships, thereby avoiding the additional role expectations that would accompany such connections. A study conducted by the Barna Group reported that "61% of pastors admit they 'have few close friends.'"[4]

What I have just described sounds like a hopeless dilemma: we need relationships, relationships imply roles, roles can lead to role conflict, which leads to broken relationships. So, you might ask, why bother?

Because we really *do* need each other. The negative cycle need not be inevitable. We can deliberately choose to build healthy, strong relationships. We can become more socially aware, learning to recognize role conflict and working to prevent it or respond appropriately when conflict arises.

In family systems terms, social awareness involves attunement to the relationship dynamics in the system, including pressure by the system to maintain the status quo or equilibrium. Relationship management includes differentiation, the ability of the individual to establish and maintain a separate identity while remaining a connected part of the system.[5] The truly differentiated pastor can prevent role conflict by proactively working to define his or her role with collaboration and input from significant others. The clearer the role definition, the more easily the pastor can manage future conflicts when they arise.

Differentiation

In many ways, differentiation is synonymous with setting boundaries. Through boundaries you declare, "*This* is me and *that* is not me," as opposed to attempting to adapt to every voice telling you who you should be. The self-discovery and self-definition work described in earlier chapters provides a foundation for and facilitates the process of self-differentiation.

Differentiation enhances your clarity and objectivity about the separateness between your self and others. This allows you to define boundaries in terms of what *is* and *is not* your responsibility. Well-differentiated individuals know that they bear responsibility for their own choices and actions, which implies accepting responsibility for the consequences of their behavior as well. Self-differentiation allows no room for blaming others or manipulating others to meet your needs, but calls on the best in you to consistently and effectively manage relationships, which is the fourth domain of emotional intelligence.

Knowing what is not your responsibility is a key aspect of differentiation. Ministers, by nature and by role definition, care for many other people. You journey with parishioners through daily events, relationship conflicts and shattering traumas. You have accepted God's call to "Rejoice with those who rejoice; mourn with those who mourn" (Rom. 12:15). Of necessity, caring for others involves situations that generate anxiety. What you, as the pastor, choose to do with that anxiety will critically impact the outcome of your interactions with others and affect all the relationships in your life.

If you are poorly differentiated, you will absorb the anxiety of others, which escalates the overall anxiety throughout the system. In many situations, people either deliberately or unconsciously hope to shift their load of responsibility onto the pastor's shoulders. If you accept that load, you will assume that you need to fix the situation to relieve the anxiety. This will increase the person's dependency on you and weigh you down with a burden that rightfully belongs on someone else's shoulders.

On the other hand, if you are well-differentiated, you can remain a nonanxious presence in the midst of tension, crisis, and conflict. You may experience anxiety, but you don't let that control you or dictate your interactions with those around you. You don't automatically or frantically accept every responsibility that is handed to you. This differentiation immediately helps others in the system resist the anxiety as well. A good guideline to follow is that we are called to help others when their loads become overwhelming (bearing one another's burdens) but we are not responsible for carrying each other's daily loads.

To set healthy boundaries requires being honest—with yourself and with others. Your boundaries must be uniquely yours. As the expert on yourself, you know your limits—your energy levels, your abilities and resources, and your competing commitments.

Christy,* a seminary student, told me about a recent experience in the church where she serves as youth pastor. Several teens approached her after the Sunday morning service and asked her to drive them to a local mall where they could have lunch and hang out together for the afternoon. Christy told me, "I knew that if I said yes I'd feel taken advantage of later on. So I said no." Christy knows the limits of her time and energy and she knew she needed time alone that afternoon. So she set a boundary. The teens tried to convince her to change her mind, but she held firm.

Christy went on, "The next week, they asked again. This time I said yes because I knew I could do it and enjoy the time with them." Setting boundaries enabled Christy to say no, but boundaries also allowed her to freely say yes at the appropriate time.

In turning down the teens' request, Christy honestly acknowledged her limits to them. Sometimes we hesitate to set boundaries because we don't want to admit that we can't do it all. We perpetuate the myth of Super Pastor, who can be everything to everyone.

Some people find boundary setting easier than others. This is another area where your self-assessment (chapter 2) can be helpful. The Thinking/Feeling scale of the Myers-Briggs Type Indicator looks at what you consider in making decisions. If you are a Feeler, a person who makes decisions based on values and feelings, you may hesitate to set boundaries for fear of hurting someone's feelings, even when the other person is clearly in the wrong. If you base decisions primarily on logic—a Thinker—you will tend to find limit setting the right thing to do and thus not a major struggle for you.

Well-meaning Christians may challenge you when you set boundaries. Rick* was hospitalized after an emotional breakdown. The doctors said that his condition resulted from stress. They warned that he needed to cut back on his activities or he would likely collapse again. Rick told his pastor he had decided to resign his position on the church council and at least take a break from teaching his Sunday school class. The pastor encouraged him to reconsider, saying, "God's word promises that you 'can do *everything* through him who gives you strength'" (Phil. 4:13, paraphrased).

Only God knows how many stress-related illnesses and even deaths have resulted from that one verse, taken out of context and used as a tool of manipulation and shame. When we read the verse in context, we see that Paul stated that God had empowered him to be content in need or in plenty, whether he was well-fed or hungry. Paul acknowledged that God provided strength in every situation. Paul did not say that he (or anyone else) should take on every available task to demonstrate or test God's strength. Setting boundaries is actually an act of good stewardship whereby we wisely use the gifts God has given us.

Boundary-Setting Guidelines

Over the years, through my own experiences and those of others, I have learned two important overarching guidelines about setting boundaries. First, boundaries that are set *with love* are much easier for others to accept. Remember, differentiation means staying connected at the same time you define your self as an individual. Sometimes when people are just getting started in this process they say things like, "How dare you even ask me to do that?" or they adopt hurtful tones of voice. With practice, you can learn to set boundaries in ways that communicate, "For my well-being (or the good of our relationship), I have to say no to that request." We can learn to set limits gently yet firmly.

A second guideline is that the best time to set boundaries is at the beginning. Our daughter, Karla, had a very wise first-grade teacher. On the first day of school, the teacher had a large poster on the classroom wall. On that poster were five basic rules for the class. Each day the students read the poster aloud together and discussed what the rules meant. At open-house night, the teacher explained to the parents that she found it helpful to start the year with strict classroom rules. She explained that she could always ease up as the year progressed, but that if she started without rules, she could never become more strict if necessary over the course of the year. To this day I still remember that rule number one was, "Keep your hands, your feet, and other objects to yourself"—we repeated it often at home that year, too! Boundaries set at the beginning of the year provided clear guidelines for the whole school year.

Your interview with or appointment to a new church is the time to begin conversations about your role and the boundaries inherent in the role. Self-differentiation is a lifelong process that impacts every relationship. It is never too late to start. If you haven't set boundaries yet, the best time to start is now.

Blessing

David said of God, "You will fill me with joy in your presence, with eternal pleasures at your right hand" (Ps. 16:11). If you are not feeling joy today, perhaps it is in part because you have not established appropriate boundaries. A life without boundaries squeezes out our relationships with those to whom we should be the closest. A boundary-less life squeezes out God. Perhaps your joylessness is because of damaged, weakened relationships. Learning how to define yourself as an individual while building healthy relationships with others frees you to experience the joy God offers. Self-definition takes the form of many small acts of boundary setting and honest personal communication.

In the next chapters, we will look specifically at your relationships at home, in the church, and in the community. David affirmed the joy of relationship: "How good and pleasant it is when God's people live together in unity! . . . For there the Lord bestows his blessing, even life forevermore" (Ps. 133:1, 3).

Assessment Journal

1. Write the names of people with whom you talk about matters that are important to you.

2. What is your relationship style? Are you an extravert or an introvert?
3. How does your list in question 1 match up with your interpersonal relationship needs? What might you change? What is really working for you?
4. Make a list of all the roles you occupy.
5. How have you seen role conflict in your life? How have you responded?

5

Relationships in the Family

Jesus asked, "What good is it for you to gain the whole world, and yet lose or forfeit your very self?" (Luke 9:25). A pastor might paraphrase that question and ask, "What does it profit if I save the whole world yet lose my own family?" As pastors, our relationships with our immediate families form a foundation that affects all of our human relationships.

Family can serve as the pastor's greatest support system and source of encouragement; family may also be a place of refuge in the storms of ministry. The pastor's family who is neglected or, even worse, actively wounded by the pastor can become a source of pain and ultimately undermine the pastor's ministry.

In his book *Generation to Generation*, Edwin Friedman explores the dynamics of family systems in the church.[1] He maintains that the pastor is part of three family systems. The first, and perhaps most obvious, is the pastor's own family—spouse, children, and family of origin. The second is the church, the family of God, as a system. Third, Friedman believes that every family in the church considers the pastor as part of its family system. This consideration carries the benefits of inclusion and connection but may carry the costs of unrealistic expectations and intrusions.

The Pastor's Marriage

If you are married, your relationship with your spouse is, and needs to remain, the primary human relationship in your life. As such, you need to live out your marriage with integrity, practicing and living out at home what you preach in the pulpit. No marriage, even that of pastor and spouse, is perfect because marriage consists of two people who are not perfect. However, *everyone*—your family, your church, and your community—benefits when you invest in making your marriage healthy and strong.

Clergy family life is frequently characterized as living in a fishbowl. Dan Reiland, author of the monthly e-newsletter *The Pastor's Coach*, likens the pastor's marriage to having your home perpetually on the real estate market: people come into your home and go through your closets at will.[2] They say nice things about you, but at the same time look for problems to justify rejection or a lower offer. Whether you like it or not, people watch the pastor's family to see how family members interact and handle the stresses of life. Perhaps this adds credence to Friedman's third point. If every family in the church sees you as part of their family, then your personal life *is* their business.

An important awareness in family systems thinking is that whatever happens in one system impacts all the other systems in which we live. What happens in your personal family system cannot help but affect your church system. How will others listen to you if they don't respect your family and marriage relationships?

I have made a startling, somewhat disconcerting discovery: most of what I do in ministry each day could be done by someone else, perhaps even better than I do it! However, the same is not true at home. Being Keith's wife and my children's mother are unique relationships that deserve and require priority in my life.

Carolyn Cutrona, professor of psychology at Iowa State University and director of the Institute of Social and Behavioral

Research, cites several studies in which at least 75 percent of married men say that their wives are their greatest source of emotional support.[3] Her statistics point to the great value of investing in strengthening a marriage and not taking that support for granted.

After years of working with clergy couples in crisis, David and Vera Mace characterized their observations of the relationship dynamics as a cyclical pattern: If one's marriage is not rich and fulfilling, being a loving person is difficult, which makes being an effective pastor difficult. The ineffective pastor becomes increasingly frustrated with the work of ministry, which in turn feeds back destructively into the marriage. They concluded, "Therefore, working to achieve a loving and creative marriage is a task of major importance" for the clergy couple.[4]

I have taught marriage and family counseling courses for years. One day following a discussion on divorce, a student, himself divorced, came to talk with me. "You know," he said, "my ex-wife and I used to attend Trinity* Church." Many years earlier, the pastor of Trinity Church had gone through a very public divorce. "I'm not saying it's their fault," he went on. "But after they split, six or seven couples in the church went through divorce not long after. It was like, if the pastor and his wife couldn't keep it together, why should we try so hard to stay together?" If the pastor's marriage breaks, the ministry will suffer and others may use that as an excuse for their own failure.

Invest Time

Time invested in relationships has no substitute. Arguments over quality time versus quantity time are fruitless because they are based on a false dichotomy. Your calendar and your checkbook indicate your values and your priorities. No one else will do this for you; you need to guard the quantity of time you share with your family by setting boundaries.

A pastor's wife once told me, "My husband spends a good amount of time with the family, but although his body is with us his mind is still at the church." You will enhance the quality of your time together as you truly attend to your mate and your children.

Joseph,* the senior minister of a three-hundred-member congregation, had a full calendar. Most weeks found him at business meetings over breakfast and lunch every day and at social events several evenings. His wife and children seldom saw him except at church. Joseph expected the same time commitments from his associate, Pete.* But Pete refused to miss family dinners on a consistent basis. He faithfully carried out his responsibilities but firmly resisted pressure to shift his priorities.

For years I taught a research course that included basic statistics. I used a simple verbal survey with the class to get some numbers with which we could play. I would ask questions like "How many times do you wash your car in a year?" As each student responded, we recorded the number on the board, then calculated the mean, mode, median, and standard deviation of all the answers. One of the questions on the survey was, "How many times have you seen a movie in the theater in the past year?" Students would close their eyes and concentrate, some counting on their fingers as they named films they had seen. Lynn* startled me by sitting up straight and raising her hand instantly. She firmly stated, "Fifty-two." As the class stared in surprise, she went on, "Every Tuesday is date night. My husband and I go out for dinner and a movie. Nothing interferes with date night, so it's fifty-two." A ministry couple and parents of teenagers, Lynn and her husband had prioritized their marriage. Date night was simply one evidence of that priority.

You may be thinking that your children's activity schedule or your church calendar is too unpredictable to block out the same night every week. So make it a different night each week. The choice of days doesn't matter. The regular prioritization *does* matter. You have to plan it and keep to your plan to make it happen. Get your children's school calendar and make plans to participate in scheduled events and maximize their holidays.

Date nights also need not be expensive. If a restaurant and theater don't fit your budget, plan to take a long walk in the park, go out for ice cream, or linger over lattes in your favorite coffee shop. What matters is your time together. As another student told me, "Date night helps us remember why we like each other."

Intimacy comes in a variety of types or dimensions.[5] Time alone together as a couple builds emotional intimacy and may lead to physical or sexual intimacy. These types of intimacy enhance the quality of the marriage relationship.

But not all couple time is exclusive. You and your spouse may be involved in activities together. Some of the richest times that my husband and I experience as a couple are those times we spend with other people—sometimes just socializing and other times working on projects. We have been privileged to travel, attending conferences together (increasing our intellectual intimacy level), and speaking together (a vocational intimacy). Building closeness in a variety of dimensions strengthens the relationship and broadens the foundations of intimacy in marriage.

Establish Boundaries

In one study, 80 percent of pastors indicated that ministry had affected their families negatively.[6] The greatest cause of this negative impact often is congregational expectations of the spouse.

I recently met with a group of pastors' wives. They came from at least four different countries and cultures. I asked them, "What do your churches expect of you?" Through a translator, one woman said emphatically, "They expect me to be involved in everything." Unrealistic role expectations are a universal problem. This same woman went on and said with a frown, "My husband puts pressure on me, too."

This dear woman felt abandoned by her husband. She needed him to support her and empower her to set boundaries, yet she saw him as demanding more of her than she felt able to give. You need to talk openly with your spouse about your expectations for your mate's role in the church, and you also need to listen to your spouse's perspective about his or her role in the church. Then you can establish boundaries together. Karen Zurheide, pastor's wife and author, wrote, "Thankfully many churches today are allowing pastors' spouses—and families—to live their own lives. But it's up to you to make your expectations clear. . . . Secure your spouse's support—communicate and agree about your role in the church."[7]

Your boundaries will look different from those of another pastor and spouse because they should be based on your spouse's interests, personality, gifts, and growing edges. Many pastors say they want to protect their mates' limits, but they subtly (and perhaps unconsciously) undermine them. Over the years, I have learned not to volunteer Keith when I find out about a need he might fill. I ask him later, privately, if he would be willing to take on that task and allow him to offer if he so chooses. We have also learned not to agree to new responsibilities when we are asked in a public place, like the foyer of the church, where we feel pressured to say yes. We agree to talk about it later and decide freely. In this way, we seek to empower each other to say no when necessary.

One area in which your spouse needs assurance of your protection of boundaries is in the realm of what I call public information. This means that you agree not to share private information about your spouse in public without his or her approval. Sermon illustrations and public prayer requests are perhaps the most common means of boundary trespassing. This isn't necessarily done deliberately or maliciously. Sometimes the pastor is by nature a very transparent person. "My life is an open book," she may reason, "so my spouse's life should be, too."

My parents experienced the difficulties of crossing boundaries with public information during my mother's illness. For the last twenty years of her life, my mother suffered with the symptoms of emphysema. As the disease progressed, she endured frequent medical appointments and occasional emergency hospitalizations. When she had to miss church, my father would ask for prayers for her, which was important to both of them. However, my mother often complained because he shared details that she felt should be private. "It's *my* body," she would protest, "and I don't want you talking about it with everyone else." She was trying to draw a boundary.

As a pastor, my husband made countless hospital calls and I often accompanied him. After a brief visit and prayer and before we left, he would ask the patient two essential questions: "What would you like me to tell your friends at church?" and "How should we pray for you?" These empowered the patient to set information boundaries.

In my teaching and writing, I often use stories about my family. Occasionally I have felt "checked" and have stopped myself from using a sensitive illustration because I didn't have permission to do so. At other times I have prefaced the story with, "I've heard Keith tell this story in public, so I know I'm not breaking his confidence."

The time and attention we devote to each other strengthen our marriage and, in turn, improve our ability to minister to others. The boundaries we establish and maintain provide security for our marriages. This truly is the working out of the vows we made to "love, honor, and cherish . . . as long as we both shall live."

The Pastor's Children

Pastors' kids—PKs—often face stereotypes in the church and in society. Many adults who grew up in pastors' homes carry wounds from the unfair expectations of perfection or the hurtful behavior of church members. Some resent the church for the time their parent was away from home or for the significant childhood events their parent missed. Yet, other PKs grow up loving the church and find themselves serving in ministry as adults. They may have fond memories of the extra grandparents and aunts and uncles the church gave them.

After years of teaching pastors and seminary students, I am convinced that much of the PKs' attitudes toward the church, both while they are growing up and as adults, is shaped by their parents. Children's attitudes are influenced by what parents give them and what they keep from them.

Give Your Time and Attention

Remember Pastor Joseph and his associate, Pete? Pete signed up to be a coach for his son's T-ball team. When Joseph discovered this commitment, he chastised Pete in a staff meeting for "prioritizing a game over God's work." Following the meeting, a wise retired pastor who volunteered on staff took Pete aside. He affirmed the younger man for his commitment to his family. Someone once said that on his deathbed, no one ever wishes he had spent more time at the office. Pete worked hard in his ministerial role, but he refused to sacrifice his family in the process.

As our children were growing up, family dinnertime was sacred for Keith and me. We made it our aim to eat together every night, even if the time had to change to accommodate someone's scheduled activities. While we ate, we talked. We often asked each other, "What is the best thing that happened today?" If a special event had occurred, we would ask, "What did you like best about it?" Now that our children are grown up and married, we still look forward to long conversations over the dinner table.

Everything I have said about making time for your marriage could be repeated here in relation to your children. Attend their school events. Cheer for them when they take part in sporting events and performances. Take time to shoot hoops or play games with them.

As with couple time, family time may include participating in church activities together. One of my sweetest memories of my son at about six years of age involves a church remodeling project. As I worked with sharp grown-ups only tools, scraping old carpet off the cement floor, Jason worked nearby with an octogenarian named Sammy Aschenbrenner. The two of them picked up scraps of carpet and tossed them into the trash can, then wheeled the trash together to the dumpster outside. We were working together, in God's house, with God's family, making memories.

Give Them Adopted Family

My children knew the blessing of many extra grandparents, like Sammy. We encouraged those relationships. My parents lived nearly two thousand miles away, so it was a special blessing when Lester, a retired pastor and friend, volunteered to go to the elementary school with the kids on Grandparents Day. To this day, several former parishioners tell us that they pray for our children and grandchildren daily. We tried to help our children see parishioners as caring for them, even when their concern took the form of criticism or correction.

Linda,* who had two grown daughters, approached Kendi*, the pastor's teenaged daughter, following the worship service. "Honey, don't you think that skirt's a bit too short?" she asked. Back in the parsonage, Kendi's parents pointed out to her that Linda loved her and was worried about how others might view her. She spoke out of sincere concern. On the other hand, if Linda had chosen to talk to others *about* Kendi, criticizing the way she dressed, perhaps questioning her morals, such critique would not be productive or appropriate. The pastor would be wise to address such gossip and protect Kendi from damaging criticism.

Give Them Boundaries

Protect your children from unrealistic expectations that others might try to force on them. Keith and I often speak about clergy self-care at gatherings of pastors and their spouses. We talk about the importance of setting boundaries to avoid burnout. At one such meeting, I noticed a woman at the edge of the group. The reason I noticed her was that she looked so tired—actually worn out. Her shoulders slumped and she had thin, sunken eyes with dark circles. She listed all of the things she did in her church. She said, "What you said sounds good, but I can't do that. I've tried saying no to things, but then people have started to ask my sixteen-year-old daughter to do them. I have to protect her, so I can't say no any more." Her husband was afraid that people would be mad at him and force him out if his family said no, so he wouldn't protect his wife and daughter either.

We need to protect our families and to empower them to protect themselves. This pastor would have done well to sit down with his wife and daughter and discuss the issue of church involvement openly. They could have talked about their strengths and gifts, then listed all the things they were currently doing. They could decide together what they wanted to do to serve God and the church, then begin practicing how to say no to new requests. The three of them would agree that if one said no, the other two would neither try to convince them to change nor volunteer each other for work in the church.

Give Them Ministry Opportunities

Help your children discover their strengths and develop their gifts. While you need to protect your children from unrealistic expectations, you can also teach them the value and joy of serving God through the church. You can lead them to set realistic expectations of their place in the family of God. Encourage them to try new things and to participate in activities according to their interests.

Our daughter, Karla, has loved to cook since she was big enough to stand on a chair in the kitchen and "help." When she was ten years old, our church underwent a major renovation project, primarily done with volunteer labor. Women from the church signed up to provide dinners for the workers at the site so they wouldn't have to waste valuable evening hours going home to eat. Karla signed up for her own turn to provide dinner. She prepared homemade lasagna and served it to the work crew. The meal was a time of affirmation of her gifts and of her servanthood. Today as an adult, she is often called on to cater church dinners, and she still finds fulfillment in serving God and the church this way.

Do *Not* Embarrass Them Publicly

The same principles about public information that apply to your spouse also apply to your children. No one needs to know when your son begins shaving, when your daughter has her first period, or when either of them fall in love for the first time. Yet, I have known pastors who revealed those things from their pulpits. It should not surprise those pastors when their children don't want to come to church and face people who know their private lives so well.

Do *Not* Give Them Your Junk

One Christmas, my husband and his siblings fell to reminiscing about churches their father had pastored while they were growing up. One asked, "Dad, why did you leave ___ church?" Their father told them of several painful situations and attacks from unhappy parishioners. The two oldest brothers looked at each other in amazement. "We had no idea!" Although they had been teenagers at the time their father faced this opposition, they had been spared the load of knowing about it. No negative words about the troublesome parishioners were spoken in the home. This left the children free to love the church; all four siblings are actively involved in ministry today.

Too many pastors' children carry an adult load of knowledge. They hear church members' failings and faults discussed at the dinner table. Give your children the gift of innocence. Allow them freedom to love and respect people in the church, even if these parishioners have brought you pain. Your children learn soon enough that their heroes are human.

Do *Not* Demand or Fake Perfection

"Dysfunctional family" has become a buzzword and is often overused and misunderstood. The most helpful explanation I have found is that all families have problems and all family members have faults but functional families deal with those problems and faults. Dysfunctional families ignore them or even magnify them.

Dan Reiland encourages pastors to give themselves and their families the benefit of the doubt and allow them to be human. However, he also reminds them "This is not an excuse for sub-biblical standards: Leaders are required to live by a higher standard, (See 1 Timothy 3) but that does not mean you aren't entitled to make mistakes."[8]

Your congregation will watch to see how you handle people and situations that are less than perfect. Eric Reed, managing editor of *Leadership* journal, writes, "If pastors try to present the image of a perfect family and act like they don't have any problems, they're so far removed from where everybody else is. Your struggles can endear you to your congregation, that is, how you battle through the tough times together."[9]

All that I have said about the pastor's family could be summarized in two statements of advice:

- Let your spouse and children be themselves, as God made them.
- Encourage and help your spouse and children to be their *best* selves.

If you keep these guidelines in front of you daily, you will be more likely to make decisions that build your family relationships and nurture your loved ones. Your ministry will also be enhanced. You will also do well to remember one caution: you don't have to meet *all* of your family's needs. No one person can (or should) do that for any other person. You can help them find places where they can have their needs met.

I often talk in my classes about the importance of nurturing clergy families and allowing our families to be authentic. One day Daniel* came to me after class with tears in his eyes. He explained how lonely his wife was and how guilty he felt. She was a full-time mom, at home with two very young children in a new city; he had two part-time jobs plus school. No wonder she was lonely. After some brainstorming together, Daniel and his wife decided that they would make some adjustments. He changed his work schedule to provide couple time. They also wisely acknowledged that they needed to find a church home where she could meet other young moms, develop friendships, and be nurtured spiritually in Sunday school and Bible study. Once they found a church where they felt at home, the family of God helped to meet her needs for support and friendship.

Single Pastors Have Families Too

The most recent data released by the U.S. Census Bureau reveals that the majority of households in the United States are now headed by unmarried adults.[10] This report reflects an increase in divorced adults choosing not to remarry, yet it also reflects a trend among young adults to postpone marriage or to reject it altogether. At our seminary, we have seen an increase in the percentage of single students over the past decade. This increase has caused us to address some of the unique issues for single pastors and seek to prepare them for some of the potential difficulties they may face.

Matthew,* a single seminary student, was in his last term when he went to interview with a church board about the possibility of becoming their pastor. Matthew was a bright student, well-liked by faculty and students. Never married, he maintained strong ties to his family. The church where Matthew interviewed was a long distance from where they lived and from where any of his friends were serving as pastors.

An older woman on the church board asked a very wise question. She said, "We know that we cannot meet all of your social needs within the church. As a single person, how will you find the social interaction you need?" This opened the door for Matthew to share his interests and to explore with them what opportunities their community offered that matched his interests.

Matthew accepted the call to become the pastor of this loving congregation. As a graduation gift, they sent him a care package filled with information about special events and must-see places in town, as well as gift cards to local merchants to introduce him to his new home. They also included telephone calling cards so that he might stay in touch with his parents and siblings.

This congregation understood that their pastor already had a family, the one into which he was born, and they encouraged him to remain closely connected to the family. They also recognized that Matthew would need an extended family in town. He needed people nearby with whom he could socialize without pressure to be the pastor, relationships that would nurture him.

Single pastors tell me all too often that church members assume they have no life outside the church. They hear subtle demands like, "Well, since you have no one waiting for you at home, I'm sure you won't mind being the last one to leave and lock up, will you?" Blessed is the single pastor whose church leaders recognize his need to create a family and the importance of protecting time for those relationships, just as the married pastor protects time for spouse and children.

Many single pastors have found a family—usually not someone from their congregation—of which they have become a part. Cindy* became the pastor of a small church comprised of families and older couples. She was warmly accepted and grew to love her congregation. She also experienced loneliness and felt isolated as the only single woman in this tiny rural area. After much prayer, she met a female pastor from a nearby city who had been in ministry for several years. This woman became Cindy's mentor and sister in the faith. Her husband and children welcomed Cindy as one of the family, and she found refuge in their home in times of loneliness.

Family of Origin

We all have a family of origin. The reality is, no matter how old we are, we continue to be influenced by the families in which we grew up. If you are married, you have two families of origin impacting your life. According to family systems theorists, we "function in all systems (areas where we live) based upon what we learn in our families of origin."[11] Problems in our families carry over into the church. Because our "first families" influence our present ministry, we need to acknowledge that influence and optimize it.

Differentiate from Family

Even in the healthiest of families, the process of a child growing up and leaving the nest represents a developmental crisis. As children become adults, family members renegotiate their roles in each other's life. I recall conflicting emotions as our oldest child graduated from college and began life in her own home and in her new career. I was proud of her accomplishments and trusted her preparedness to take care of herself. Yet at times I wanted to help her too much with my advice, and I grieved that she no longer needed me. On several occasions as tension rose between us, I said for her sake and mine, "Please be patient. Your father and I are new at this grown-up-child thing, too."

Our children needed to differentiate from us, just as Keith and I had done with our families years earlier. Differentiation requires work, emotional energy, and open communication. Attempts to avoid differentiating result in confusion and tension. Darlene* found herself torn between her husband and her parents. Her husband, a seminary student, worked part time in a local ministry. Darlene loved their involvement in the church and was proud of her husband's work. Every week, she called her parents to keep in touch with them. With excitement, she would share what they were doing and what they dreamed of in future ministry. Her parents would respond with, "That's nice, but *this* is what you ought to do," and proceed to project a different ideal future for her.

Darlene ended these conversations defeated and confused. "I love my parents and I love my husband," she told me, "but I just can't handle being in the middle anymore." She shared her husband's vision but didn't want to hurt her parents' feelings. She needed to learn how to differentiate, to stay connected to her parents yet identify and define herself with them. She decided that she would thank her parents for their concern and let them know how much she loved them; she would also ask them to support her in the decisions that she and her husband made. If necessary, she would explain to them how conflicted she felt when they gave her their criticism of her plans. Once she was able to do this, her relationship with her parents became more adult-to-adult and her sense of internal tension diminished.

Begin to Heal Past Hurts

Students often grant me the privilege of trusting me with their deepest hurts. Many men and women involved in or preparing for ministry have experienced painful, often horrific childhoods. They may have totally cut themselves off from their families, but they fail to realize the extent to which their family system and their past influence their present and their future.

The scope of this book does not allow for in-depth discussion on healing from family-of-origin issues. However, resources dedicated to that discussion are available.[12] If you recognize that you carry unresolved pain from your childhood or that you are repeating unhealthy relational patterns, please seek professional help in dealing with your wounds. Take advantage of every available means to come to terms with your past and to find the best relationship possible with your family of origin. Whatever this process costs you in time or resources, it will reap multiplied rewards in future relationships and ministry. What happens in the family *does* carry over into the church.

Our relationships in our families form a foundation for relationships within the church. Whether single or married, parent or childless, God has created you for relationship. May clergy families become sources of joy, encouragement, support, and strength to serve the family of God.

Assessment Journal

Answer the following questions before you go on to the next chapter.

1. How do you show that you value your spouse?
2. How do you protect your spouse and your marriage?

3. How do you show that you value your children?
4. How do you protect your children from church members' inappropriate demands?
5. After reading this chapter, what changes do you intend to make in the way you relate to your family?
6. If you are a single pastor, who makes up your family? What will you do to meet your needs for connection and social support?
7. Are there issues you need to resolve in your family of origin? If so, what steps will you take to do so?

6

Relationships at Church

"Here is the church and here is the steeple. Open the doors and see all the people." This little hand game I learned as a child kept me quiet through some not-very-interesting-to-a-child events. As I folded my hands together and wiggled my fingers, I would actually name some of those people in my head. They were all there: my Nana and Pop-Pop; Mrs. Worthington, the organist; "Aunt" June, my Sunday school teacher; Rev. Palmquist; and all the others.

In this childish hand game, the fingers the people of the church—are interwoven. The same is true of the lives of the real people in the church. Relationships in the church affect every aspect of the way the body of Christ functions.

As ministers, our relationships with people in the church largely determine the effectiveness of our ministries. In the previous chapter, I referred to Rabbi Edwin Friedman's model of family systems in the church. As part of that model, he proposes that each individual family in the church considers the pastor as a part of their own family system. As a member of their family, most people in your congregation grant you admission into the deepest, most private places of their lives. You walk with them in their finest hours and you receive a front-row view of family dysfunctions.

Your relationships with people and your response to the trust they place in you will make or break your ministry. Consider two different pastors, Andrea* and Brad.* Both are in the first year of their first pastorate after graduation from seminary. Andrea called me one day and said, "I just love being a pastor. It's the greatest thing ever. I get to spend time with people. I can't believe the things they have told me and the awful situations in some of their lives. I'm way over my head and I don't have answers for them. But, I cry with them and love them and we pray together and it seems to help." Andrea's people know that their pastor cares for them. She sees their trust as a gift, their confidence as a privilege. Because of the relationships she has built, they will be more likely to trust her leadership in the future and believe she is making decisions that will be good for them individually and corporately.

Brad, on the other hand, e-mailed me to express his frustrations. "It's not what I expected. Oh, the people are nice enough, but they just seem resistant to every new idea I have. I've been trying to put a little life into the worship services and I've spent a lot of time trying to work with the Sunday school teachers on a reorganization of the education program. But they just seem to want to sit around and talk. I have trouble keeping them focused.

"I make hospital calls if someone's there for more than a day, and I have visited every shut-in at least once since I got here. You know that pastoral care is not really my gift, so I'm leaving most of that to the Compassion and Benevolence committee." Brad sees relationships as nonessential, secondary to the task at hand. He sees people's trust in him as a burden, not a privilege. He wants to cast a vision for the church, but he hasn't developed the social capital to have people buy into his vision.[1]

Daniel Goleman would point out that Brad has not mastered the third and fourth domains of Emotional Intelligence: social awareness and relationship management. He has failed to realize the importance of building a solid relational foundation for his ministry. Recall the old saying, "People don't care how much you know until they know how much you care." I firmly believe in the value of high quality education for pastors. To serve the church effectively, pastors need solid foundations of knowledge in theology, philosophy, Scripture, and church history and an understanding of interpersonal dynamics. But the ministry is not a choice of either knowing *or* caring. Healthy productive ministry involves both knowing *and* caring.

The Pulpit and Pew Project at Duke University Divinity School studied the life situations of men and women who left local church ministry.[2] This study identified seven main motivations for leaving local ministry. Those who left voluntarily did so primarily because of a preference for another ministry or due to a need to care for families or children. Those who left voluntarily or partly voluntarily revealed five major motivations: conflict in the congregation, conflict with denominational stances or officials, burnout (including frustration, feeling of constraint, or sense of inadequacy), allegations of sexual misconduct, or problems in their family (including divorce). All five of these motivations are relational in nature.

LifeWay Christian Resources conducts an annual study of the reasons for forced terminations of ministry staff (senior pastor and associate). For the past ten years of the study, the top five reasons have remained the same: (1) control issues (who should run the church), (2) poor people skills, (3) the church's resistance to change, (4) pastor with a too-strong leadership style, and (5) the church was conflicted before the pastor arrived. "The only difference is in their order from year to year. We consistently see the inability to develop and maintain healthy relationships within the church as the reason for dismissals."[3]

What interferes with the development of healthy relationships between pastor and people in the church? At least six factors contribute: (1) failure to build a foundation, (2) fear of friendship, (3) failure to establish healthy boundaries, (4) personality differences, (5) difficult people, and (6) fear of conflict.

Failure to Build a Foundation

When you arrive at a new church you may be eager to get started. A new vision may energize you as you see the potential in this new beginning. You want people to see that you are a hard worker, a leader of action. Especially if the transition between pastors has taken a long time, the people may be chomping at the bit to get started, too. Fred Oaks, coordinator of the Kern Family Foundation Pastoral Ministry Program, cautions that jumping into busyness too quickly can cause a relational short circuit. "Like wires conducting electricity, personal relationships conduct the energy of ministry and service. Often, new pastors and church members give relationships short-shrift in order to 'jump in and get busy.'"[4]

The wise pastor takes time to get to know people first while slowly easing into the tasks to be done. You communicate that you care about the other person as a *person*, not just about what they do in the church. When parishioners feel that the pastor truly cares about them, they feel like part of the team and view their church involvement as shared ministry. If parishioners feel that the pastor only values them for their contribution, they may see themselves as servants of the pastor and come to resent their perceived taskmaster.

Chuck Swindoll wrote about the importance of building good relationships with lay leaders.[5] He suggested deliberately planning times together between official meetings, either one-on-one or in small groups. These times may involve business, but they primarily focus on building relationships and playing and praying together. He also emphasized the importance of expressing genuine caring for individuals and appreciation for their participation in the community.

Pastors who build strong relationships with their parishioners discover that it becomes easier to deal with hard things when they come up. The relational web becomes a strong scaffolding that supports the community when tensions arise.

Fear of Friendship

For years denominational leaders and ministry experts have warned pastors and their spouses against allowing church members to become too close. Commonly accepted wisdom has been that friendships with laity carry too much risk and just don't work. Yet, following this policy has left many pastors aching with loneliness in the midst of loving congregation members who would befriend their leader if only they were allowed. How can true community develop if the leader of the community remains distant?

Friendships between clergy and laity do pose unique challenges. They create dual roles; "the pastor" becomes "friend." Any time a dual role exists challenges may arise. Those challenges need not prevent the pastor from allowing friendships with parishioners. Pastors need to acknowledge the potential hazards of dual roles and figure out how to negotiate around them.

One potential danger is jealousy. Nancy's* husband was senior minister of First Church when Dawn* and her husband first visited the church. They had lived in the neighborhood for years but had fallen away from the church and their faith—until now. Nancy's warm welcome made Dawn feel right at home. The two women quickly became close friends and realized how much they had in common. They were about the same age. Both had grown children and loved their roles as full-time homemakers. They shopped together and participated frequently in church and community projects. They talked on the phone with each other daily.

Then Susan* and her family moved to town. The young couple had three preschool children. Susan's husband had just started a new job and they had bought their first house. She asked Nancy for information on childcare and for help with home decor. Soon Nancy wasn't home when Dawn called to chat. Where once Dawn had felt secretly proud that she was the pastor's wife's chosen friend, now she felt rejected and jealous of the time Nancy spent with Susan. Dawn and her husband eventually drifted away from the church.

Nancy could have done a couple of things differently to prevent the jealousy and hurt and to maintain friendships with both women. In one congregation where Keith served as minister of music, I sang in a trio with two other women and we became very close friends. We often talked or went out for lunch together during the week. Our children played together. On occasions, the three couples had dinner together. We established two unspoken rules. First, on Sunday we didn't sit together. In fact, we rarely talked with each other then; we focused on other people. Second, when we did spend time together at church, we didn't talk in front of other people about things we had done or tell insider jokes. We tried not to do anything that might cause others to feel left out. Perhaps Dawn and Nancy's friendship would have survived if they had followed these guidelines.

Choose Wisely

You can't be close friends with everyone. Watch out for people who want to become your best friend. Some will seek to make themselves indispensable to you and then expect to be treated specially. Often they are the first to welcome you and rush to earn your confidence.

Jeren* was excited to begin his first position as a youth pastor. His first meeting with the parents had gone extremely well. He was particularly impressed with Tom,* whose son was in the junior high group. Tom had immediately made Jeren feel accepted and had even volunteered to help with the fall retreat. Tom and his wife had invited Jeren for dinner his first Sunday and encouraged him to feel free to drop by anytime after that. Surely, Tom would be a great friend and asset to Jeren's ministry with the teens, until June rolled around and it was time for summer camp. Jeren needed one more volunteer to go with the senior high boys to camp. Tom offered to go, but only if he could take his son, who was still too young. Jeren refused to make the exception. Tom responded angrily. From that point on, the relationship between Jeren and Tom was awkward.

Not everyone who befriends you or volunteers to work beside you in ministry has ulterior motives or strings attached, but some do. If you take your time and let relationships grow slowly, motives often rise to the surface. Truly genuine friendships stand the test of time and can withstand disagreements. True friendships can survive times of role clarification when you need to say, "As your pastor, I have to do this, even if you disagree." Proceeding cautiously and deliberately may help you prevent future pain and disappointment.

Share Wisely

Another challenge in clergy friendships with laity is the mistaken belief that true friends can talk to each other about anything and everything. You don't have to verbalize every thought you have ever had in order to be friends with someone. Personal friendships, even with church members, should not be based on the church. You shouldn't share gripes about church staff or other parishioners with anyone from church. Church gossip is not appropriate in any relationship.

At Duke Divinity School a group of pastors, scholars, and laity gathered to talk about friendships in ministry. One member of the group reflected on the mistaken idea that intimacy means revealing every detail of our lives. She remarked, "But Scripture never lifts that up as a good way to be. You just don't just say something that's hateful or unkind. We all have different barriers and rules we place around friendships in our lives, but that doesn't mean we can't be close."[6]

Pastors do need a place where we can vent about the stresses and frustrations of ministry. A friendship with a parishioner is not that environment. A relationship with another clergy person is the appropriate context for that. The next chapter addresses those relationships.

Let Them Care for You

Pastoral ministry implies a fiduciary, a "held in trust," responsibility for the people in your church. Many pastors interpret that responsibility to mean that they always need to act as the caregiver with congregants. They become uncomfortable when others extend care toward them. As friendships develop, caring behaviors become more mutual. Much of the tension that develops around clergy-parishioner friendships relates to this delicate balance. How can the shepherd accept care from one of the sheep?

In most congregations, you will be blessed by people who also want to care for you as part of the body of Christ. The example of Jesus's interactions with his disciples can guide us through this sensitive balance. From the time when Jesus called his disciples, until the time of his ascension, we see Jesus's friendship with his followers. He allowed them to serve him. On one occasion, a woman anointed his head with expensive perfume (Matt. 26:6-13; Mark 14:3-9). On another, a woman anointed his feet and wiped them with her hair (Luke 7:37-39). Simon Peter's mother-in-law waited on Jesus and the disciples (Mark 1:30-31). Strong bonds of friendship tied Jesus with his followers. Jesus told them, "I no longer call you servants, because servants do not know their master's business. Instead, I have called you friends, for everything that I learned from my Father I have made known to you" (John 15:15).

Jesus did not let friendship deter him from his calling. When Peter tried to deny Jesus's prediction of death (Matt. 16:21-23), Jesus rebuked him. We see no evidence in Scripture that Jesus felt obligated to grant other people's wishes just because they had acted lovingly toward him. He did not allow friendship to manipulate or seek special favors. When the mother of two disciples, James and John, sought a special place for her sons, Jesus denied the request (Matt. 20:20-23).

In an article for *The Christian Century*, Rev. Lillian Daniel wrote of the time when her mother died.[7] Four church members flew to Washington, D.C., to sing at the funeral, representing the congregation on that day. She invited them to stay for the reception following the service. After a brief hesitation, they agreed on one condition: that she would not feel any responsibility for them on this day. She did not need to introduce them to others or make sure they had refreshments; she only needed to let them care for her. She had found true friends in her congregation.

Failure to Set Healthy Boundaries

Sometimes pastors resist setting boundaries because they fear that people will not like them. The self-differentiated pastor must balance the need for relationship and connectedness with the need for self-definition and identity. The differentiated pastor helps develop a healthier church, and the differentiation of laypersons creates a healthier congregational family. Ron Richardson suggested that differentiation is "caught" when modeled for others: "But any movement toward differentiation by anyone in the congregation will have a positive impact on each of the other members in the church. Churches, and individual members, do not progress much further toward greater differentiation than do their leaders."[8] Thus, any efforts you as the pastor make toward defining yourself more clearly will help your congregation do so, which will positively impact relationships on all levels.

One of the most visible ways you can model self-differentiation is by your refusal to enter into emotional triangles. In so doing, you can remain a nonanxious presence in the midst of tension and relational conflict. An emotional triangle can develop when two individuals (Person A and Person B) experience growing tension in their relationship. Each person comes to you and tries to convince you to side with him or her against the other. Both apply pressure, expecting you to resolve the issue. The pressure may increase if one of the two is a friend and expects your "loyalty" because of your friendship. You in turn recognize that you are responsible for your relationship with Person A and for your relationship with Person B, but that you cannot be responsible for the relationship between them. Only they can resolve their conflict. You can assist them—together—in the process if necessary, but you cannot and should not assume responsibility for it. This pastoral model also teaches Person A, Person B, and any onlookers how to maintain boundaries. As you assume a self-defined position, you challenge others to do so by example. Self-differentiation assists you in dealing with the challenges of dual roles.

If you sense high levels of anxiety in your parishioners, you can offer resources and training experiences directed toward self-differentiation and understanding emotional processes.[9] You might make these tools available to pastoral staff, board members, Sunday school teachers, and other lay leaders, either in groups or individually. You can also encourage differentiation in your preaching ministry. You probably won't use the word *differentiation* but you can preach on godly character, taking responsibility for one's self, and living according to one's convictions. According to Thomas Fischer, "Directives against anger, teachings regarding reconciliation and forgiveness, exhortations to patience and being able to 'walk through the valley of the shadow of death' yet fear 'no evil' (Psalm 23) are but a sampling of the nonanxious, self-differentiating content of Scripture."[10] If you do the hard work of self-definition and guide your congregation to increasing levels of self-differentiation, you will reap the benefits of leading a spiritually and relationally healthy community of believers. You will also reap the benefits of healthy friendships within that community.

Teaching others to self-differentiate includes helping them to set boundaries. Lauren's pastor failed to help her in this way. When I met Lauren,* she was in the hospital following a suicide attempt. As we visited, I could quickly see her commitment to God and to the church. She had been deeply involved in church as far back as she could remember; her family life revolved around the church calendar. She ticked off on her fingers the positions she held in the church: Sunday school teacher, mission society president, head of the kitchen committee, member of the choir, youth activities director, women's ministry coordinator, and participant in a host of other one-time events. She held thirteen job titles in the church!

As she neared the end of her list, Lauren began to cry. "I just couldn't keep doing all that. I'm exhausted. And I'm not doing anything very well right now." She had gone to her pastor and told him how she felt. She related to him her fear that she would totally fall apart if she could not lighten her load in some way. He responded, "I think I can find someone else to take care of the kitchen committee for a while. But I *really* need you to continue in the other areas. No one else can do them quite as well as you do." Lauren didn't have the courage to just tell her pastor no when he needed her so badly. She had reached a point where death seemed the only way out. Lauren desperately needed to be taught and encouraged to set boundaries and self-differentiate. For her, it became a matter of survival.

Lauren's story is based on a real person with whom I worked. Few overworked laypersons will attempt suicide but many may develop stress-induced illnesses such as ulcers, high blood pressure, or overwhelming fatigue. Others may leave the church or passive-aggressively fail to fulfill their commitments while they smile sweetly and say, "I'm so sorry. I have so much on my plate I couldn't get to that."

The pastor can teach others to set boundaries by modeling in two ways: saying no to overcommitment and saying yes to those practices that nurture (see chapters 9 and 10 for more on this subject). Pastors can also help parishioners create boundaries by assuring them that it is OK to say no and avoiding any subtle pressure for commitment.

Personality Differences

One of the advantages of investing time in building relationships is that you discover people's strengths. If you do this before you plunge deeply into new programs and activities, you can help people find those places of ministry that fit them best. You can focus on matching gifts and abilities with needs rather than just filling job vacancies with warm bodies.

As you become better acquainted with people you may find that a certain person or persons just seem to irritate you. If you choose to follow your natural human inclination to avoid people with whom you don't feel in sync, you may miss out on a great friendship. Instead, if you consider personality type you may discover that the other person is not trying to defy you or undermine your ministry; they just think differently than you do. That very challenge faced Pastor Greg* as he assessed his reaction to Eric, a member of the congregation.

Pastor Greg could hardly wait for the meeting to start. He had worked with members of the music committee for weeks to put together a plan for a Christmas pageant and tonight they would present it to the church board for approval. The chair of the music committee made the presentation. Around the table, eyes lit up and people nodded affirmatively. The committee chair had barely finished when Eric's* hand shot up. "Pastor, how can we afford this pageant? There will be costumes and extra lighting and all kinds of costs!" Heated debate followed and the meeting ended without a final decision for or against the pageant.

Greg trudged home, fuming inside. "Eric does this at every meeting. I'm tired of having him shoot down every idea I propose." Once Greg took time to calm down, he began to reflect, "Maybe Eric has a point. We really hadn't thought through the budget carefully." This young pastor had found Eric to be a man of integrity, careful with details in every area of his personal life. Perhaps he wasn't just trying to make the pastor's life difficult, but he wanted to be as careful of church finances as he was of his own personal budget. Actually, Eric could probably help the music committee work out a realistic, affordable plan for the pageant to be presented at the next board meeting.

Don't allow personality differences to divide you from the people in your congregation. Value those differences. See them as they really are: gifts from God, and the building blocks of the family of God.

Difficult People

Sometimes no matter how hard you try, you will encounter someone you can't get along with. Certain people seem determined to destroy the church and tear down pastoral leadership. Responding to such attacks appropriately is essential, protecting the church from such poison with all the power inherent in the pastoral position. Dealing with these difficult people is beyond the scope of this book, but I mention it for two reasons.

First, I want to assure you that these attacks, at the root, are really *not about you*. Even if you were the perfect pastor, these people would complain, find fault, and undermine you. They may spread rumors and lies about you. For some reason, either relational dysfunction, a history of trauma, or a personality disorder, they have become destructive. You may not be able to "fix" them, but you can and should seek to deal with them assertively to protect yourself and your congregation from their harmful behavior.

Second, I want to direct you to resources that address the issue of dealing with difficult people more in-depth. Several books have been written. *Never Call Them Jerks: Healthy Responses to Difficult Behavior* by Arthur Paul Boers, *Antagonists in the Church: How to Identify and Deal with Destructive Conflict* by Kenneth C. Haugk, and *Clergy Killers: Guidance for Pastors and Congregations Under Attack* by Lloyd Rediger, which I also recommended in the introduction to this book, are good examples of available resources. Enos Martin, a Mennonite bishop and professor of psychiatry, and E. A. Vastyan, an Episcopal priest and professor emeritus, have written an article to help pastors recognize the signs of a person with borderline personality disorder (BPD) and to equip the pastor to help these persons without allowing them to create havoc in the church community.[11] The person with BPD is typically a female with a history of childhood abuse who uses a lot of all-or-nothing thinking and is extremely disruptive and demanding.

Louis McBurney, psychiatrist and founder of Marble Retreat Christian Counseling, has written about how to handle a person with a passive-aggressive personality.[12] Whether or not you currently have such an individual in your congregation, you will likely find this material helpful in your ministry. In seminary classes, I have asked students to define *passive-aggressive*. Typically, no one offers a verbal definition but many smile knowingly. They don't know how to put it into words, but they see a face in their minds—they know a passive-aggressive person in their family or church. Webster's defines *passive-aggressive* as a person or behavior "characterized by disguised resistance to the demands or expectations of others, that is expressed in hindering progress, as by procrastination, stubbornness, or inefficiency."[13] Such an individual can cause great disruption in the church and difficulty for the pastor.

Fear of Conflict

Whenever you put two or more people together, no matter how healthy or self-differentiated they are, you can expect to have conflict eventually. The only way to avoid conflict is to isolate yourself. But life alone on a desert island gets lonely at times. To choose to build relationships implies choosing to experience conflict. Sometimes conflict arises in church because of disagreements about role expectations or personal preferences. Sometimes personality styles clash. Even the different ways we respond to conflict can cause more conflict.

We learn how to deal with conflict by watching our parents and other significant adults while we are growing up. When my parents were angry, they raised their voices, but we kids were never allowed to yell back. I learned to fear shouting and I still feel my stomach tighten at the sound of loud, angry voices.

In some homes, everyone speaks loudly, often all at the same time, to make their points with each other. Loud voices aren't threatening to these people—they are simply conversation. To relate to shouters, I have had to learn to face conflict head-on without cringing (at least outwardly). It is a price I am willing to pay for relationships.

So, conflict is inevitable and conflict is normal. The ability to deal with conflict constructively is a lifelong growth process. I would suggest a few basic guidelines drawn from the example of the early church's response to conflict and found in the New Testament.

Listen to Each Other

You cannot resolve conflict without communication. When you disagree with someone, you need to work doubly hard to understand that person's position. Once you have listened well, you can state your position. Real communication occasionally results in an "ah-ha" moment and the issue is resolved through understanding. However, even if the conflict is not settled in the process, listening to each other then frees you to decide how to handle the disagreement.

Agree to Disagree

No matter how much they listened to each other, Paul and Barnabas would not agree on what to do with John Mark (Acts 15:36-41). So they agreed to go their separate ways, each convinced they were right. They apparently parted as brothers and did nothing to undermine each other's future ministries. Ultimately, the church grew as a result of their multiplied impact.

Work It Out

In some cases the source of conflict is an issue so essential that we cannot agree to disagree. The question of whether or not to require Gentile believers to undergo circumcision was such an issue. The story is told in Acts 15:1-30. Paul and Barnabas brought the issue to the church leaders. Everyone had a chance to voice their positions and to relate their experiences of God's work. "After much discussion" (v. 7 NIV) a decision was made which settled the conflict. All agreed to live by the decision of the Jerusalem Council.

Past Congregations

One reason some pastors and their spouses shy away from friendships with parishioners is fear of the inevitable goodbye. One pastor's wife complained, "It never fails. We've been here three years. I'm finally feeling at home, I know my way around town, and I've made some friends in the church and the neighborhood.

Now, we're moving again. I'm not sure if I can do it—starting over again."

You have pastored this congregation for years. You have baptized their babies and buried their dead. Together you have laughed and cried, fought and fellowshiped. But last Sunday you announced your resignation. You and your spouse have prayed and sought wise counsel. You know this move is the right decision. You are excited about the new doors of ministry that have opened. But that is next month. This month you have to deal with the goodbyes.

Any change entails saying goodbye to the former things. Friendship ties that develop between pastor and parishioner don't automatically evaporate when the pastor moves. The relationships that have developed over time in close proximity need to be renegotiated over geographical and ecclesiastical distance. The process of redefining relationships can be painful, awkward, and threatening, but ultimately enriching.

Painful

Any change taking you to a new place means leaving the old. Leaving implies grieving. You realize all that you will miss—the good times you have shared and the future things that you will not do together now. When Keith announced to our church that we would be leaving so he could attend graduate school in another state, we were flooded with dinner invitations. Everyone who had ever intended to have us over but had "not gotten around to it" simply *had* to spend an evening with us in the last three weeks before we moved. The same thing has happened every time we have moved. In part, these invitations are an attempt to put off the final goodbyes.

When we moved to our present home to teach at the seminary, we not only left our congregation but family as well. Our adult children, Keith's parents, siblings, and several nieces and nephews all lived in the town we were leaving. We spent time together, laughing over memories and knowing how much we would miss each other. Perhaps the most wrenching moment came as we pulled out of the church parking lot on our last Sunday, with our car loaded for the three-day drive to our new home. I will never forget the image of Keith's 83-year-old mother waving goodbye from the doorway. Goodbyes are painful.

Awkward

Once we have moved, maintaining relationships with former parishioners can be awkward. Is it still OK to ask personal questions now that I am not their pastor? How much contact is enough? How much is too much? Should I call to ask how the surgery went or should I leave that to the new pastor who has visited them in the hospital already?

When Barbara Brown Taylor resigned her pastoral ministry to begin teaching, she remained in the same town. In her memoir, *Leaving Church*, she describes the experience of encountering former church members while running errands around town: "After I left church . . . cruising the aisles at the Winn-Dixie, I did not get the same looks that I was used to . . . we treated one another as gingerly as onetime lovers who had resolved to remain friends."[14]

Some of the awkwardness comes because we are not sure what to talk about. Perhaps remembering our friend role can be helpful; still maintaining our friendship, we can talk about what friends talk about—our lives, our families, and our experiences. We are no longer in the role of our friend's pastor, so talking about church business would be inappropriate.

Threatening

Many former parishioners fear that they will hurt your feelings if they like their new pastor. They may feel disloyal to you. You can encourage them to make a healthy transfer of their loyalty to the new pastor if you can truly state that it need not threaten your ongoing friendship.

You may also feel deeply saddened if your former church member reports negative things about the church's current state. You may fear that the fruit of all your earlier efforts are now threatened. Your natural reaction may be to start giving advice and warnings. Instead, remind yourself that it is God's church, not yours. Tell your friend that you are sad to hear their news, but you will pray with them and not try to fix it. You might even have to ask them to not bring such reports in the future, as it is too painful.

Enriching

When all is said and done, at least a few people from every congregation in which you serve will likely remain lifelong friends. These are the people who could call you today and—even if you haven't talked in years—you could pick up right where you left off, as if you had never been apart. These relationships are just a few of the rewards of effective ministry. During the Christmas season, we experience the blessing of receiving cards, letters, and photos from, literally, around the world. They come from former parishioners and students who have become friends as we labored together to serve God and the world that God has made. These deep friendships are a rich reward for our ministry.

Assessment Journal

1. What factors have kept you from developing relationships in your church?
2. What have you done to build a foundation of relationships in your church?
3. How would you describe your level of self-differentiation?

4. What boundaries have you established in your church relationships?

5. How have you seen personality differences with others affect your ministry? What type of person bugs you? What does that person have to offer that you need for balanced ministry?

6. How do you respond to conflict?

7. How have you managed relationships with former parishioners?

8. In light of your reading in this chapter, what changes do you intend to make in your interactions with current or past parishioners?

7

Relationships
in the Community

Joel* walked down Main Street, whistling. He had come to this small town just a few weeks ago to become the pastor of First Church—"the little stone church," as everyone here called it. After growing up in big cities, Joel was beginning to get used to the idea that almost everyone in town knew each other. He had decided that he liked the cozy, friendly atmosphere of this place.

He nodded in greeting as he passed a woman he didn't recall ever having seen before. "Good morning, Pastor," she said cheerfully.

Joel stopped. He smiled hesitantly and asked, "I'm sorry, but I don't recall having met you. Do you attend First Church?" She introduced herself as Sally and assured him that it was alright that he didn't remember her. No, they had not met, so he could not be expected to know her name, but she knew he was the new pastor in town. "Since you don't attend First Church, feel free to call me Joel," he said politely.

"Oh, no," she replied. "Even though I don't go to your church, you're still our pastor in this community. I'll call you Pastor. Have a great day."

Pastor to the whole town! Joel had just experienced a massive dose of pastoral identity.

What does it mean to you when someone calls you *Pastor*? Wherever you go, you carry the image of pastor with you. According to Rev. William Horton, Joel should see the community as an integral part of his ministry. In an article in *The Expository Times*, Horton wrote, "Community involvement is a Christian imperative. . . . Our faith gives pastors no encouragement to believe that the corporate aspect of their ministry is to be exercised solely within the fellowship of the church. The world beyond that fellowship must equally be their concern, because it is God's concern."[1]

Even in larger cities where the minister might not be identifiable in the crowd, the church has an identity; the community often has expectations of congregations and their leaders. When I went with a group of students to New Orleans, we were studying pastoral care and trauma response. Our goal was to offer a pastoral presence in the community as an extension of one of the local churches. The director of our denominational emergency response program gave me a stack of florescent yellow T-shirts with "Restoring Hope" and "Disaster Response" printed on them in bold black lettering. He advised, "Give these to the team. If you're out in the neighborhood, wear them. People recognize these shirts and they'll know you're with the church; they'll know you're OK." The shirts identified us with the church's image.

We knocked on doors in the neighborhood and said something like, "Hi, we're here with Disaster Response and the church on the corner. Do you know Pastor Larry? We're just checking in with folks to see how you're doing." After a while, we would ask if we could pray for them. Often people came out of their houses, grabbed our hands and said, "Oh, yes, please pray. That's the only thing that will help right now!" and they proceeded to share their needs with us. Their response told us that, although we only touched their lives for a few moments, we ministered God's grace to them. The identity of the church and the expectations of the pastor in the community opened the door for those moments of grace.

Pastor to the Whole Community

William Horton proposed that the pastor's involvement in the community is not a personal, individual responsibility, but that the role of the pastor is to act in a representative way, sharing the ministry of outreach with the whole congregation. The pastor can accomplish this by both inviting the community to be involved in the church and facilitating the church's involvement in the community.

Nelson Granade, in his book *Lending Your Leadership: How Pastors Are Redefining Their Role in Community Life* identifies three biblical roles—prophet, priest, and king—as informing the ways a pastor may serve the community.[2] On different occasions the pastor may function in any one of these three roles. All three are valued and needed by the community. So, the pastor need not choose *either* one role *or* the other, but find ways to do all three at the appropriate times.

Prophet

The prophetic role is one of truth telling. The prophet sees abuses in the community and speaks out against them, calling people to live according to God's standards. Perhaps the most visible public prophet in recent United States history was Rev. Dr. Martin Luther King Jr., who spoke out eloquently against the sin of racism in our society. Rev. Dr. Marie Fortune, founder and senior analyst of the FaithTrust Institute, is a present-day prophet.[3] She uses all of her skills and power to bring the hidden sins of sexual and domestic violence out into the open and exhorts the church to make a difference.

The pastor-prophet calls people to accountability, challenging both congregation and community to seek God's direction in all things. Granade warns that some pastors have mistaken *prophetic* for *judgmental,* assuming that God had chosen sides in our moral debates. He states, "Genuine prophecy, however, does not trap God into one view or another, but recognizes God's transcending power to change the view of all. When God speaks, it is usually not to say that one is right and another is wrong, but to point all to a higher ethic."[4] Our communities need men and women who boldly speak God's truth into the problems that surround us.

Priest

If the prophet's role is to afflict the comfortable with God's message, the role of the priest is to comfort the afflicted with God's grace. The priest ministers as counselor and keeper of liturgical tradition or ritual.

Sometimes the priestly function takes on a more formal, official air. During our son's senior year of high school, the school board decided that they could no longer sponsor the traditional baccalaureate service for the graduates. Citing their fear of crossing separation of church and state boundaries, the board told the students that if they wanted to plan a service, they could use the auditorium, but the school would not officially sponsor it.

The teenagers wanted to continue the tradition of baccalaureate. They wanted a worship service in which they could express their commitments to God and thankfulness for God's provision thus far in their lives. The graduating class appointed a committee; four of them were pastors' kids. The father of one of the graduates pastored a church just down the street from the high school. They asked him to speak at the ceremony. Pastor Cliff served as a priest that night for a group of high school seniors and their families. Opportunities to pray or offer spoken tributes at public events arise as people in your community know you are available to serve.

As you get to know the people of your community, you will uncover many hidden opportunities for the exercise of the priestly function. One day while our seminary class was in New Orleans, we stopped to refuel the bus. When I went into the gas station to pay, I greeted the young woman behind the counter and asked how her day was going. She must have recognized that my question wasn't simply polite small talk, because she actually told me about her day. She told me about working two jobs to support herself and her ailing grandparents with whom she lived. She talked about fighting with her parents and trying to take community college classes in her "spare" time. While my students waited outside, I served as priest in the gas station, listening and praying for this hurting woman.

Pastor Jenny has embraced the role of pastor to her community. When she heard that a local teen had died in an automobile crash, she hurried over to the high school and offered to help in any way she could. She wrote to me, "Almost all I did that day was listen, although a few students asked me if I would pray with them, which I did. It was heart wrenching. . . . The teens' body language gave a pretty strong indicator [of] whether they wanted to talk or be alone, and I just attended to that. . . . To be honest, to me it was just part of being a pastor."[5]

King

We often think of power when we hear the word *king*. A certain degree of power—the ability to influence and lead others—is inherent in our identity as pastors. In recent years, we have heard so many public stories of church leaders who have abused their power that we tend to shy away from or deny our power. But power is part of the reality of the pastoral office. We would do well to acknowledge it and determine to use it well, to determine to use our power alongside of and for the people we lead, and not to use our power over or against them.

Nelson Granade calls the pastor to accept the kingly role and the power that it entails. He suggests four responsibilities of governing power. They are to protect the people, to unite people, to adjudicate legal disputes, and to ensure proper stewardship of shared resources. Pastors who have gifts, training, and experience in leadership and administration have much to offer their greater communities in a kingly role.

Pastor Claudia* didn't set out to become a community leader. She just wanted to be a good mother and stay informed about what was happening at her children's school, so she went to PTA meetings. Claudia was the kind of person who never met a stranger—a clear extravert with a strong interest in other people. She wasn't afraid to speak up in meetings to ask questions or to make suggestions. After a year of active participation, Claudia was elected president of the PTA and reelected to that position annually until her youngest child completed elementary school.

From this position of leadership, Claudia was able to spearhead several projects, including cleanup and renovation of the playground to make it safer for the children. She used her role to advocate the needs of children and families in the community.

Claudia's role in the PTA made her more visible in the neighborhood and it opened doors for her to get to know the ministers in other churches around town. She worked to bring her clergy colleagues together and eventually they planned a community-wide interfaith Thanksgiving service. This became an annual tradition with church leaders rotating and sharing responsibilities each year. One congregation would host the service, the pastor from another church would preach, another pastor would lead prayer, and everyone was invited to sing in a mass choir. The shared service was an outward sign of the unity that Claudia sought to build among spiritual leaders in her community.

Putting It All Together

As I said, when the pastor considers these three roles in the community, it is not a question of either-or but of how to do both-and. For example, several years ago, my husband attended a workshop on conducting English as a Second Language (ESL) ministries. Several people from our congregation stayed for a long time after the session talking about the need for such a program in our church. In a prophetic voice, Keith finally said, "Enough talking. What are we going to do about it?" He researched demographics and discovered that 3,569 people in our city of 100,000 people spoke English "less than well" according to census data. Seven-hundred-three households were linguistically isolated—that means that no one in those households spoke English. Keith spoke the truth to our congregation, challenging them to ask how God would have them respond in grace and love.

Keith then used his gifts of administration and took the pastoral role of king. He explored teaching resources, funding options, and space needs and managed the arrangements to begin an ESL program. He recruited teachers and planned a training session.

Once classes began, Keith took on a more priestly role. Each week he affirmed teachers, cheering their successes and listening to their concerns. He talked to the students and helped them in many ways, explaining a utility bill for one man and assisting another with a job application. One night he helped two boys with math homework that their mother couldn't understand because the directions were written in English. Keith officiated over the graduation ceremony and celebration we had at the end of each year in his priestly function as celebrant and leader of ritual.

Open Doors in the Neighborhood

Rev. Fred Rogers, an ordained Presbyterian minister, was more commonly known as Mr. Rogers, television friend of millions of children. Every day he would greet the boys and girls with a song inviting each one to be his neighbor.

Your community may not sing you an invitation, but open doors await you. Your community needs your participation and expects your leadership and that of your church members. As a matter of fact, some of your parishioners may be way out ahead of you in the arena of service to the community. The identity of the church as a body of believers involved in their community seems to be more than an expectation. It is a social reality, supported by statistical evidence.

Robert Putnam, in his book *Bowling Alone,* reported on research that indicates the weakening and collapse of social and civic organizations across the American landscape.[6] He noted one significant exception to this trend: the involvement of what he called "religious adherents" in their communities is still strong.

Nearly one-half of all personal philanthropy and volunteering in the United States takes place within a religious context. People who worship regularly or say that religion is very important to them are much more likely to participate in all areas of civic life. Whether the voluntary association is political, social, athletic, academic, or self-help in nature, "it was membership in religious groups that was most closely associated with other forms of civic involvement."[7]

Each religious leader needs to find his or her unique role in the community. The best place(s) for you to serve depends on your personality style, strengths, and gifts and should be consistent with your family life and ministry goals. The examples of Rev. Marie Fortune, Pastor Jenny, and Pastor Claudia suggest a few avenues of service you might consider. You may find other open doors through agencies such as public safety departments, public schools, sports organizations, medical facilities, and funeral homes.

Public Safety Departments

Public safety departments such as police and fire departments often look for men and women to serve as chaplains. Our friend and pastor Dwight would often be called out to the site of an accident or a fire as chaplain of the local fire and rescue unit. At the time of the tragedy, he would offer a priestly presence to the families involved. He also ministered to the rescue personnel after they assisted at traumatic scenes.

Public Schools

With school budget cutbacks, volunteer help in the visual arts, music, and physical education may be welcomed. Pastor Jenny's church building sits directly across the street from the elementary school in town. Her parishioners have chosen to offer an after-school program including tutoring, games, and snacks, especially for those children who would otherwise go home to an empty house. In other communities, church leaders might volunteer in classrooms or for special assemblies and field trips.

Sports Organizations

Our involvement in community sports grew out of our children's activities. To be more involved in their lives, we attended countless softball, volleyball, basketball, and soccer games and wrestling matches. Our participation in the parents' booster club opened the doors to many relationships and ministry opportunities. The opportunities involved all three roles of prophet, priest, and king at different times. Perhaps the most visible role Keith filled in those years was when he officiated at the funeral of a seventeen-year-old girl, a friend of our family, who died when her car crashed into a tree. At her funeral, the church was filled with several hundred teens that had seen us around the school and now heard Keith speak God's message. He served as priest and prophet to the community that day.

Medical Facilities

Medical facilities like hospitals and nursing homes often welcome volunteer chaplains. Too often residents in care facilities are forgotten, and the church only seems to remember them at Christ-mastime with a poinsettia plant and a strolling group of carolers in the hallways.

Funeral Homes

A funeral home in your community may need pastoral services from time to time. Pastor Tom had conducted services at the lo-cal funeral home after several of his parishioners died. The funeral director asked him if he would be willing to provide a service for a family who had no pastor to call on in their time of loss. He agreed, thinking this would be an occasional avenue of ministry to his community. His ministry has proven to be such a blessing to others that some weeks he has as many as three funerals. He meets with each family in preparation for the service, then leads the service, and makes a follow-up contact with the family, fulfill-ing a priestly role for those who grieve.

You can see that the opportunities to serve—the open doors— are limitless. You can give to the community as much as your gifts and your time allow.

So far, we have focused on what *you* can give in relationships outside the church. One very important gift that your community may offer to you is the gift of clergy colleagues and friendship. With other clergy you can share certain things you can't talk about with anyone in your church. Only another minister can truly understand some of the unique pressures you face.

At Duke Divinity School's Theological Colloquium on Excel-lence in Ministry, participants emphasized the importance of friend-ships to sustain the pastor in long-term ministry. Becky McMillan, associate director of Duke's Pulpit and Pew, asked focus groups of pastors what they needed. Pastors responded that what they really needed were "mentors and confidantes, people with whom they could feel safe confiding their flaws, people who would hold them accountable and contribute to their spiritual formation."[8]

This kind of friendship goes way beyond small talk over coffee. Pastors' support groups too often degenerate into gossip sessions and competition over statistics. Truly supportive clergy friendships require an atmosphere of emotional safety to match the accountability. This kind of relationship doesn't just happen—you need to seek it out. Ask God to lead you to colleagues you can trust.

Supportive clergy relationships *can* be maintained over a distance. I know of several women who serve as pastors in churches in four different states. They all went to seminary together and became true friends. They stay in regular contact via e-mail and call each other if unexpected problems arise. If one of them has a problem, she knows her friends will understand and support her through the tough time. The connection these women share is especially important to them because several of them have no local female colleagues.

Yet, at times it seems there is no substitute for a real person—present, not just over a phone line or on the other end of a computer connection. I recently talked to a pastor who told me about the greatest gift God had given him: two clergy colleagues in his town. They were all from different denominations. Their theological differences didn't detract from their shared love of God and the church and their shared need for a safe place to be real about ministry. They have met together once a month for eight years. This pastor had recently discovered that both of his friends would be moving this summer. He had begun grieving already: "I can't imagine surviving ministry without their support and that outlet. I'm already praying that God will send others to take their place in my life."

Gary Kinnaman was a pastor racing toward burnout and depression. Gary met Alfred Ells, a counselor and organizational consultant, when his church was in a crisis. With Al's help, Gary not only survived the crisis but also developed a Pastors in Covenant group that sustains him to this day. These two men have cowritten a book about their experience and their model for small help groups entitled, *Leaders That Last: How Covenant Friendships Can Help Pastors Thrive.*[9]

Many other resources exist to help pastors develop clergy relationships. Many models have been proposed. The model you use isn't critical. The support and accountability that you experience *are* critical. If you are not currently experiencing a peer collegial connection, do everything within your power to make it happen. Seek out colleagues. Initiate contact and begin building trust today. God has created us for community and we really *do* need each other.

Assessment Journal

1. In your journal, make three columns with the headings Prophet, Priest, and King. Under each heading, identify ways in which you already serve (or have served in the past) your community in that role.

2. What doors of opportunity are open to you in your community? Where might you make yourself available for ministry?

3. How well do you know the other ministers in your community? Have you found colleagues with whom you might establish a deeper supportive connection?

4. What steps will you take to build the supportive collegial community you need to sustain you for long-term ministry?

8

Danger!

Recently, I was sitting at the airport waiting for a flight. Trying to use my time wisely, I grabbed my cell phone and returned several calls for work. Near the end of the last call on my list, I heard the telltale beep—"low battery" flashed on the phone screen. No problem, I thought, I could just plug it in at a nearby outlet until they called my flight. Oops! I had forgotten to pack the charger cord. Now what would I do? There were power outlets all around me, but I had no way to tap into them.

I was on my way to speak at a conference. The three-day meeting was being held within an hour's drive of both my children and their families, so I would have the bonus of family times. Both Karla and Jason have fully embraced cell phone technology and their homes have no landline phones. The retreat center where I was speaking had no public phones available. My cell phone was my link to them and to the outside world for the next five days. I needed to recharge the battery somehow.

Many pastors live their ministry lives in a perpetual state of low battery—in danger of losing power completely and no longer functioning. Perhaps this imagery can help us understand the reports of the high numbers of pastors who leave ministry, whether permanently or for extended leaves of absence. Pastors often allow their connection with God to weaken, a critical concern considering that they represent God to their parishioners and to the world. Healthy pastors, on the other hand, nurture their relationship with God. Recognizing the source of power for ministry, they are empowered as they nurture their spirits through spiritual formation and sabbath practices. Michael Zigarelli, associate professor of management at Charleston Southern University, pointed out that Proverbs 3:5 and Matthew 6:33 tell us to trust God and lean not on our understanding, seeking God's way first. "It follows, then, that *obstacles to our relationship with God are also obstacles to leading God's way.*"[1] In this chapter we will consider three obstacles that interfere with the pastor's relationship with God, tripping up many pastors in their efforts to lead God's way.

Busyness

Jesus told the parable of the sower (Luke 8:5-15) who planted seeds into a variety of soils with varying results. Some of the seeds fell among thorns that choked them out. "The seed that fell among thorns stands for those who hear, but as they go on their way they are choked by life's worries, riches and pleasures, and they do not mature" (v. 14). The thorns that threaten pastors may not be worries about riches and pleasure but about planning worship services that will please the crowds and attending to the needs of the saints. The end result is the same: God's word is crowded out of our lives. We are cut off from the very source of our spiritual life.

Most pastors are extremely busy people. In earlier chapters, we have looked at the expectations and goals you have for yourself in ministry and in relationships with others. We have considered the expectations others have of you. All of those expectations constitute a lot of good things for us to do. One of my students wrote, "Pastors get so caught up in doing the things of God that they neglect becoming the person of God they need to become."

Michael Zigarelli referred to busyness as a disease of epidemic proportions. He conducts ongoing research on spiritual issues, gathering data through his Web site, Assess-Yourself.org. One-hundred-sixteen clergypersons responded to his Obstacles to Growth Survey.[2] Nearly two-thirds (64 percent) responded affirmatively that "busyness gets in the way" of developing their relationship with God.

Dr. Daniel Spaite, director of the emergency medical department at the University of Arizona trauma center and a pastor's son, warned pastors of the dangers of becoming need focused rather than "Father focused" in their ministries.[3] Spaite referred to Jesus's prayer in John 17:4: "I have brought you glory on earth by finishing the work you gave me to do." Clearly, Jesus did not meet *all* the needs of *all* the people around him while he was on earth, yet he had completed the work his Father had given him. There was no sense of a frantic, last-minute attempt to focus on and keep meeting needs. Jesus focused on his Father as the source of his to-do list.

We Affirm Busyness

In a paradoxical way, we like our busyness. Oh, we complain about it a lot, but we also seem to find our value and a sense of self-importance in our hectic schedules. "They need me," we assure ourselves. We think, "No one else could do it quite as well as I will" as we write one more obligation on our calendar.

We even applaud each other for our overload. We say things like, "I don't know how you do it. I thought *I* was busy!" When was the last time you heard someone complain that they had too much free time? Have you ever congratulated someone for taking a sabbath or for going on a spiritual retreat? No, we honor those who are busy, usually by asking them to take on one more responsibility.

Busyness Becomes Familiar

We become accustomed to the pace we keep. We equate accomplishment with value. At age sixteen, I had learned this lesson well. Heavily involved in church and school activities, I had little time for sleep. I proudly told my concerned mother, "I would rather burn out for Jesus than rust out." I hope it is wisdom, and not just age, that has caused me to change my pace somewhat since then.

We pastors may not know what to do with ourselves when we slow down. We know how to manage and administrate programs and how to provide pastoral care for those who suffer. But we often have not been taught, or had modeled for us, how to grow spiritually and lead others spiritually. So we continue to do what is familiar and perpetuate our busyness.

Busyness Allows Us to Hide

Our hectic schedules demand attention, so we don't have time to think about our failures or grief. We use busyness like a drug that numbs us to the messy, painful places in our lives. To be healthy, we have to detoxify ourselves from the drug of busyness to allow our real selves to surface. Only then can we really address our pain and find healing. We cannot grieve our losses until we remain still long enough to realize them and feel the emptiness they create. We cannot really grow until we acknowledge our failures and growing edges—our real selves—and open our lives to God's healing grace. All of these processes take time and honesty, which requires that we cease our hectic striving and find the pace that God has ordained for our lives.

Study versus Formation

Pastors are uniquely vulnerable to the temptation to substitute study *about* God for spending time *with* God and allowing God to form them. This can be a major obstacle to spiritual growth. I coteach a course with the impressive title of "Personal and Spiritual Development of the Minister." We require that all incoming master of divinity students take this course. Among our course objectives is that the student would develop the "ability to pursue holy character (Christlikeness) by practicing faith formation and the classic Christian disciplines as means of grace." The class meets weekly, and a portion of the time is spent in small groups. The groups are encouraged to pray together and decide on certain disciplines that they will practice over the span of the semester together.

One group excitedly told me that they had decided to memorize Scripture together. Several admitted that they had not done so since they were little children in Sunday school. A couple of weeks later I asked how it was going and was surprised at their answer. The memorization project had failed. That part didn't totally surprise me, but their conclusion did: "We realized we are all very busy between work and school. We have so many pages to read and we're studying scripture and theology and stuff all the time. We have decided we need a 'theology of enough.' Instead of feeling guilty for not doing spiritual disciplines, we're going to say that what we read for school is enough." This group of pastors-in-training were trying to convince themselves that they only had time for *either* study *or* a devotional life, but not both.

In reality, the pastor needs to hold the two in balance with study on one side of the scales and devotional life on the other. We need the study of Scripture, theology, and church history to truly teach and lead the church well and to provide solid spiritual food for our parishioners. We also need vital devotional lives—fresh, daily interaction with God through prayer and Scripture—to keep our own spirits alive. Without this dynamic personal time with God, our teaching and preaching loses power and effectiveness. Our spirits become as dry and lifeless as the desert breeze.

I encouraged the students not to settle for "enough," but to press on for the best. Rather than establishing separate, restrictive rigorous devotional reading programs for themselves (which had become onerous), I encouraged them to think of the balance. Whenever they read Scripture for course work, I challenged them to also spend time in prayer, asking how God would have this Scripture shape their lives. When they read a theology text, they could spend time meditating on how their reading applied to their own life and experience. *Both* study *and* spiritual formation are essential for a vital Christian life and ministry.

Self-Reliance

Self-reliance is implicitly at the root of both busyness and neglect of our spiritual formation. Saying by my actions that I am too busy to take time for God implies that I don't need God in order to do all the things I am so busy doing. Zigarelli looked at the relationship between busyness and leadership style. He concluded that "a lifestyle that crowds out God culminates in the self-sufficient practice of leadership."[4]

One of the dangers of self-assessment and awareness of our gifts and strengths is the tendency for some people to think, "God is pretty lucky to have me on the team." Some ministers, especially those who are very charismatic, can make a pretty good show of ministry on their own power for a while, but ultimately what we have to offer is not enough. Parker Palmer wrote that burnout develops when we try to give what we don't have: "Burnout is a state of emptiness, to be sure, but it does not result from giving all I have: it merely reveals the nothingness from which I was trying to give in the first place."[5]

I am not suggesting we adopt a "worm theology" or deny the gifts and strengths that God has given, but we must acknowledge the source of all the goodness in our lives. We must recognize how miniscule our best is when compared to the riches of God's glory and power. Why would we want to settle for what we can do with our finite selves—our limited abilities, time, energy, knowledge, and resources—when God "who is able to do immeasurably more than all we ask or imagine" (Eph. 3:20) desires to work in and through us.

Overcoming the Obstacles to Relationship with God

The first step in connecting to the source of power for ministry is to overcome our self-reliance and acknowledge our dependence on God. Our accurate and ongoing self-assessment reveals our limitations and our strengths. God-reliance requires recognition that God is the source of every good and perfect gift (James 1:17) and that we depend on God for everything we have. We offer it back to God in ministry.

Connect to the Source

The natural result of affirming my need for God is to seek God and draw closer. I cannot be content with simply studying God's word, but I seek to be formed by it. Jesus affirmed our need for connection when he said, "I am the vine; you are the branches. If you remain in me and I in you, you will bear much fruit; apart from me you can do nothing" (John 15:5). We must remain in Christ, the source of life.

Keith and I have a clematis in our backyard. Every summer the vines grow ten feet or more, then beautiful purple flowers open up along each branch. Every fall the branches turn brown and dry out. My neighbor, an experienced gardener, has taught me to prune those vines way back in the fall so they can grow up strong the next spring. A few years ago, I didn't get the pruning done before winter set in. I looked out at the plant one day and realized that every stem had broken off—snapped by the Kansas wind—just above the ground. I was sure I would never see another purple flower. The plant was dead. Then came April and time to clean up the yard. I discovered about a dozen new shoots coming up from the base of that vine. The life source was still there and the flowers did bloom that summer as beautiful as ever.

Jesus, the vine, gives life to us even in the harshest of climates and circumstances. We must remain in him. One thing that Jesus said in this passage is that the gardener prunes the vines. The reason for pruning is to remove the dead wood and those stems that are least productive so that all the energy of the plant goes into the most productive branches and the best fruit.

Prune Your Busyness

When we acknowledge our dependence, God will prune our lives if we allow it. That includes our calendars and to-do lists. As we seek to be focused on God in our ministries and our daily lives, God will reveal to us those activities that are dead wood and should be cut away. God will also show us areas of life that produce healthy fruit and others that simply drain our energy and should be trimmed off. When God prunes your life this way, you will discover you are no longer too busy for God. You realize that you need time with God in order to give God's best to the work you do.

My cell phone would not work without a power source. I could study the owner's manual forever but that would not charge the phone. All the phone's past busyness and usefulness halted until I pulled up to the electronics store, bought a recharger cord, and connected the phone to the electrical power. My connection was restored.

For all Christian believers, spiritual growth cannot be just one more thing added to our lives. Allowing God to form us must be *the one* thing—the center of our lives. For men and women in Christian ministry, God must be at the center of our lives, not only for our personal formation and health but also for the benefit of all those who call us pastor. Father William from Holy Cross Abbey in Berryville, Virginia, said, "The congregation as a whole cannot grow in faith beyond that of the pastor."[6] May we lead the way in full dependence on God and commitment to God's kingdom.

Assessment Journal

1. How have you allowed busyness to choke God out of your life?
2. What might God want to prune out of your schedule?
3. How is your balance between study about God and formational practices?
4. At what times are you most likely to rely on yourself for the work of ministry?
5. What makes you most aware of your need for God?

9

The Care and
Feeding of Your Spirit

Everywhere you look these days, it seems that someone wants to give you advice on how to be healthy. Bookstores devote entire sections to health or diet and nutrition. Fitness centers open in every new shopping center. Magazine covers promise "Lose ten pounds in ten days—without starving yourself!" We hear television commercials for fitness waters and diet plans, for sleeping medications and better mattresses for healthier sleep. My morning newspaper today had a feature article on exercise classes for five-year-olds! I guess you are never too young for the marketers.

Underneath all the advertising language and gimmicks, plans that effectively promote health share three basic components: balanced nutrition, regular exercise, and adequate rest. These three factors are the building blocks for physical well-being; they also are essential for spiritual well-being.

Just as our bodies need food, exercise, and rest, our spirits need their equivalents. Peter encouraged believers to "crave pure spiritual milk, so that by it you may grow up in your salvation" (1 Pet. 2:2). In his first letter to the Corinthians, Paul used the imagery of running a race and challenged the believers to go into training and prepare themselves spiritually for the race of living the Christian life (1 Cor. 9:24-27). The writer to the Hebrews promised, "There remains, then, a Sabbath-rest for the people of God" (Heb. 4:9).

Good physical health and development doesn't happen automatically or by accident. We must attend to our bodies and make wise lifestyle choices to nurture them. Similarly, spiritual health and maturity doesn't just happen. Apparently, the Corinthian believers thought it would just happen. Paul challenged them to grow up, saying that he still had to feed them spiritual milk—baby food! We must attend to our spirits and deliberately discipline ourselves as we seek good spiritual food, devotional exercise, and sabbath rest. Spiritual disciplines are those behaviors that draw us closer to God, helping us to grow more like Christ in our daily lives.

All of the other relationships in our lives are enriched by this growing relationship with God. As we love our Creator, we can appreciate who we have been created to be in God's image. As we love God, we are able to love others with God's love, to see them as God sees them—created in God's image.

Yet, like little children, many of us chafe at the idea of discipline. The word may conjure unpleasant memories of doing what someone else wanted you to do. Actually, we don't engage in spiritual disciplines for anyone else's benefit. We recognize our own insufficiency and our need for God; spiritual practices help us draw closer to God. In the process, we become more spiritually mature. A healthy cycle begins to develop: the more I seek God through spiritual practices, the closer I come to God; the nearer I am to God, the more I see my need and desire to do whatever is necessary to draw even closer.

God actually gives us the desire for self-discipline. Paul wrote to Timothy, "For God did not give us a spirit of timidity, but a spirit of power, of love and of self-discipline" (2 Tim. 1:7 NIV). Interestingly, in the King James Version, the last word of that sentence was translated "a sound mind." Self-discipline is not only related to spiritual growth and health, but it is also closely related to mental health. If discipline will result in spiritual, physical, and mental wellness, then I want to practice discipline in all areas of my life—for my own good. I can embrace the word *discipline*.

Developing a Plan

Perhaps one reason we struggle so much with spiritual disciplines is that we have all read someone else's "perfect plan" for growth and tried it, only to fail. As you seek to develop your own personal spiritual formation patterns, please realize that there is no such thing as a one-size-fits-all program.

Among the wide variety of disciplines from which to choose, you will find yourself drawn to some and cold toward others. For each discipline you decide to use, you can shape your practices to fit your personality style and your current spiritual formation needs. You can and should also engage in practices that stretch you, taking you a bit outside your comfort zone to enhance your growth and provide balance. Reflecting on your self-assessment may be helpful as you consider your personal path to spiritual growth.

Your Personality Type

Your personality type affects your spiritual journey. If you are an extravert, you may find that you feel most fulfilled when you serve others. You may be more drawn to group discussions of Scripture and corporate prayer. On the other hand, introverts often are more satisfied with private times of prayer and journaling. If you are an introvert, you might find great satisfaction in quiet times of Scripture reading and meditation. The thinker may revel in theological reflection on Jesus's teachings and the Epistle writings. The feeler may love the parables and the stories of Jesus's interactions with people. Many specialists in the use of the Myers-Briggs Type Indicator (MBTI) have recognized and written on the influence of personality type on the spiritual life.[1]

How You Conceptualize God

Your spiritual type also reflects your natural preferred ways of knowing and learning about God and how you conceptualize God.[2] Corrine Ware maintains that these two dimensions of spiritual type are innate and inner directed. In Ware's model, the speculative and affective preferences for knowing and learning about God are similar to the MBTI preferences for thinking and feeling mentioned above, so the implications for spiritual formation would be similar. The second axis of Ware's model—apophatic and kataphatic—adds another dimension for understanding your spiritual type. How you conceptualize God has obvious implications for your prayer patterns. The person who takes an apophatic approach will think of God as an unknowable mystery; the writings of the ancient mystics may resonate with them. Songs and scriptures that emphasize God's transcendence will appeal to the person with apophatic thinking patterns. The person who conceptualizes God through a kataphatic lens will image God as revealed and knowable. The vision of God walking in the cool of the evening with Adam and Eve and songs and scriptures that emphasize God's immanence and caring will likely appeal to the kataphatic person.

To simplify things, we can think of spiritual disciplines as those that generally provide food (Scripture reading and study), exercise (prayer, worship, journaling, and service), and rest (sabbath). These categories can be helpful as you seek to develop a balanced approach to spiritual health. If I eat a balanced diet, but don't exercise, I will have the fuel I need to survive, but underdeveloped muscles. If I exercise frequently, but don't eat wisely, I may still gain weight and be poorly nourished. If I exercise and eat well, but neglect rest, I will still be vulnerable to illness and exhaustion. I need all three; the goal is to build toward a healthy balance. In this chapter, we will look at the disciplines that feed us and through which we exercise our spiritual muscles. In the next chapter, we will consider the essential discipline of rest, keeping the sabbath.

Good Nutrition

The first time I led a women's Bible study, I was only twenty-three years old. I had grown up in the church, never missing a Sunday service or a Wednesday night prayer meeting. I had met with Bible study groups in college, so I thought that as a young pastor's wife I was ready to take the next step and lead this group. I was ready for all the new Christians who would come and learn from me and my experience. The first week several women gathered in my living room. I don't remember exactly how many came, but I do remember two things. First, no new believers were in the group. As a matter of fact, most of these women had been in the church longer than I had been alive. Second, one of the women was Esther, a retired pastor's wife in her seventies. What could I ever teach her about God's word? She should be teaching me.

Esther did teach me—a lot. She came faithfully, carrying her well-used Bible. When she spoke, she would share about what God had taught her that week in her reading. She showed me that we are never too old or too experienced to learn more; we will never know all there is to know about God or the Bible. She had discovered the truth that "his compassions never fail. They are new every morning" (Lam. 3:22-23) and she still hungered for God's word.

In the familiar account of Jesus's visit to the home of his friends in Bethany (recorded in Luke 10:38-42), Martha scolded because Mary did not help her with the meal preparation. (Martha's obstacle to relationship with Jesus was her busyness.) Jesus told Martha that Mary had discovered the one thing needed, which was to sit at Jesus's feet and hear his words. The one thing we need today is to hear God's word.

Too often, I am afraid, Scripture reading can become perfunctory. Some people follow a schedule to read the Bible through in a year; others read a chapter of Proverbs and two or three Psalms each day. They may have a reading schedule tucked in the front of their Bible and keep track of their daily assigned reading. These patterns provide structure. I know of many people who follow them and feel that they feast on God's word every day. I know of others who see doing their devotions as just one more task to be completed. They read through the designated passages with a determined air, and check off Bible reading from their daily to-do list. They have gulped down their spiritual food without taking the time to actually taste it or digest it properly. If you find yourself in this second category and you don't feel fed after you have read God's word, perhaps you need to approach it differently. Even the best habits can become routine and lose their appeal.

I am an extravert and I have found that if I sit in a quiet place and read the Bible silently my mind starts to wander. I focus much better when I read aloud. I am also an external processor, so hearing the words helps me to think about them more clearly. I like to interact with what I have read. As a young Christian, I was taught to ask at least two questions when I read the Bible: "What is God saying here?" and "What is God saying to me in this passage?" One goal in asking questions of Scripture is to engage the whole being in your reading: your mind, emotions, imagination, creativity, and will. The practice of *lectio divina* has helped me to do this.

Lectio divina (holy reading) is an ancient practice that can be used individually or in small groups. Lectio involves four readings of the same brief passage with guided times for reflection, meditation, and prayer between readings.

Several authors have provided guidelines for lectio divina and other specific scripture-reading practices.[3] I encourage you to explore these resources. As you encounter a spiritual discipline that is new to you, you might try it for at least a week to see how it fits you and whether it will become a part of your own ongoing spiritual formation pattern.

Exercise

Prayer, journaling, worship, and service are among the exercises for your spirit.

Prayer

At its very foundation, prayer is communication with God. Communication is the lifeline of relationship, essential for growth and deepening connection. Jesus often sought out a quiet place to pray, in the process setting an example for his disciples. He taught them to pray what we have come to know as the Lord's Prayer (Matt. 6:9-13).

Most people think of prayer as talking to God. For true communication to occur, one must speak and also listen to the other speak. Too often, we don't take the time to listen to each other or to God. To the extent that we desire true communication, prayer requires solitude and times of silence. Ruth Haley Barton refers to solitude as making space for God. The psalmist David invites us to "be still before the LORD and wait patiently for him" (Ps. 37:7a). In those moments of quietness we hear the still, small voice of God.

Busyness is the antithesis of solitude and stillness. We have become so accustomed to multitasking in order to accomplish everything we "need" to do that we really struggle to focus our attention on one thing, let alone something that requires a quiet spirit. One of my roommates in college would put on headphones and play her favorite music while she studied for exams. She would tell you that the music calmed her and helped her focus on the

books, but then she would start swaying to the beat and singing along with the music. She couldn't have comprehended or
remembered much from those study sessions, and I am afraid her
grades revealed that.

Trevor Lee, in a *Christianity Today* article, suggests that our
penchant for multitasking has affected our prayer lives. We don't
discipline ourselves to give God our full attention, and our prayer
times suffer. Lee advises, "If we want to hear him, to be moved
by the weight of our petitions, or to be awed by the privilege we
have of approaching our Father, we have to be there—heart, mind,
and soul."[4] This kind of prayer, where we are fully present with
God, truly is a spiritual discipline and requires deliberate effort
on our parts. The rich reward that we find is true communion as
we enter God's presence.

Paul also exhorted the Thessalonians to "pray continually" (1
Thess. 5:17). With the exception of retreats and sabbath, few of
us can spend the majority of our time in the kind of intense prayer
that requires solitude. We have jobs, families, and responsibilities.
Surely we cannot experience solitude continually. Yet, we can
maintain a spirit of prayer even in the midst of our comings and
goings. Just as you would converse with a companion on a long
car trip, you can converse with God as you journey through the
day.

You can keep the communication line open, listening for God's
voice and breathing prayers of thanksgiving or petition throughout
the day as people or places trigger your prayers. On a typical day,
as you drive to the office, you may pass the school your children
attend or a school bus and pray for the children and their teachers.
At the office, you spend time in sermon preparation. You ask God
for guidance and listen for direction and wisdom as you meditate
on the chosen scripture passage. If you have a counseling appointment or you make hospital calls, you pray for the people you are
with and ask God to help you see them the way God sees them.
Back at the office, you prepare the agenda for the next board

meeting. You pray for wisdom and guidance as you lead. Because you are tuned in to hear God's voice, when you think, "I should call Mrs. Hughes," you take it as a nudge from God and call her just to see how she is doing today. Thus, the day is bathed in a companionship with God, praying continually. Brother Lawrence, a seventeenth century Carmelite lay brother, called this continual conversation, "practicing the presence of God."[5]

As a child, one of my best friends was the girl who lived next door. Her family was Roman Catholic, as were most of the families in the neighborhood except mine. While she was going to catechism class and making her first communion, I went to Sunday school and vacation Bible school. On occasion, she would tell me what she was learning in catechism classes and all the things she had to memorize, including prayers and worship responses. What struck me was how detached she seemed as she recited these things. She would repeat them over and over without inflection, hardly noting what she was saying. In my childish self-righteousness, I determined then and there that written prayers were dead and, therefore, of no value. No sir, you would never catch me using an old, recycled prayer that someone else had written; I would use my own words and pray from my heart.

I maintained that self-righteous attitude well into my adult years. Then I began to read some of the written prayers of the saints and realized that their words were my words. As I reflected on the Lord's Prayer, I realized that the words Jesus spoke nearly two thousand years ago are still fresh today when I really attend to my prayer. I still pray spontaneously most often, using my own words, but my heart also thrills as I read aloud and repray prayers that were written by brothers and sisters in the faith who have gone before me. Every night while our seminary class worked in New Orleans, we ended our day in prayer together. We shared stories of our pastoral contacts that day; we prayed for the people we had met and for each other. Our hearts were blessed as we concluded each evening with the petition from *The Divine Hours,* a collection of prayers based on the format of fixed-hour prayer or Daily Offices. How fitting, in a city that has seen such destruction, to ask God to watch over "those who work, or watch, or weep this night, and give your angels charge over those who sleep. Tend the sick, Lord Christ; give rest to the weary, bless the dying, soothe the suffering, pity the afflicted, shield the joyous; and all for your love's sake. *Amen.*"[6]

Journaling

Journaling is another form of communication with God. You might journal your responses, questions, and ideas as you read Scripture, making notes of things you want to study more deeply or share with others. You might also journal your prayers, actual written letters to God, along with reflections from quiet times recording the messages you received from God. Some people use their journals to maintain prayer request lists and corresponding lists of answers to prayer.

The basic principle of the discipline of journaling is that it is for your benefit and growth, so find a pattern that fits you. Some people write their best thoughts sitting in front of a computer and keep an electronic journal; others prefer special bound books to record their prayers. You might prefer to keep a folded piece of paper tucked in your Bible and put it in a three-ring binder when it is full of words. Whatever format facilitates your communication with God is the best approach for you.

Worship

Worship is a spiritual discipline that we talk about a lot but really struggle to define. In recent years, church culture has often limited the idea of worship to the music we sing in church, which has cost us much in the rich understanding of the true discipline of worship. Vine's *Expository Dictionary of New Testament Words* states that worship may broadly "be regarded as the direct acknowledgment to God, of His nature, attributes, ways and claims, whether by the outgoing of the heart in praise and thanksgiving or by deed done in such acknowledgment."[7] This expanded vision of worship resonates with Paul's words to the believers in Rome: "Therefore, I urge you, brothers and sisters, in view of God's mercy, to offer your bodies as a living sacrifice, holy and pleasing to God— this is true worship" (Rom. 12:1). True worship is everything that we do (offering our bodies) in reverence of Christ (in view of his mercy).

Often, a significant portion of our ministry responsibilities relate to regular gatherings of fellow believers for corporate worship. As a pastor, while you plan for worship times, the fundamental question becomes "What will bring honor and reverence to Christ?" and not "What will warm the people's hearts?" As you lead parishioners in corporate worship, it is easy to slip into performance mode, making sure all the details are managed and the service flows smoothly. As much as possible, seek to maintain your focus on "God, His nature, attributes, ways and claims"[8] to direct your worship to God. Avoid the habit of becoming an uninvolved onlooker as you lead others in worship.

You can also develop an attitude of worship throughout the week. Brother Lawrence spoke of a sense of awe and reverence that accompanied his awareness of God's presence in his daily life and work. He felt that he worshiped God so fully as he labored in the monastery kitchen that it was merely a continuation of worship when he was called to the chapel for formal hours of prayer.

Service

Service, according to Paul's letter to Rome, is also an act of true worship as we give our bodies to God. Through the act of serving others, we draw closer to God. Dietrich Bonhoeffer considered what he called "active helpfulness" the second most important ministry that one Christian can offer to another. He recognized the spiritual discipline of allowing ourselves to be interrupted or inconvenienced by the needs of others. He wrote, "It is part of the discipline of humility that we must not spare our hand where it can perform a service and that we do not assume that our schedule is our own to manage, but allow it to be arranged by God."[9] John Wesley, father of the Methodist movement, considered acts of mercy to be a means by which we experience God's grace.

Setting the Scene

You can do several things to enhance the impact of the spiritual disciplines in your life. Perhaps the most fundamental thing is the attitude you bring to your practices. In the parable Jesus told of the sower, the right attitude is like having the soil well prepared to receive the seed of God's work. Many pastors project the belief that they have it all together; they have arrived at spiritual maturity. They often hide behind a mask of self-sufficiency. Spiritual disciplines become for them a formality and the seeds bounce off their hardened hearts. True growth can only come when we humbly acknowledge our need.

Researchers surveyed a group of pastors that had been identified by Christian mental health professionals as exemplifying spiritual and emotional health. Two-thirds of this group cited the importance of engaging in spiritual disciplines to draw them more closely into their relationship with God. In interviews, these pastors revealed that a sense of self-sufficiency was not a primary goal for them. "Rather, they have attempted to rest their identity in the character of God, thus acknowledging their own weakness and relying on one whom they perceive to be stronger and more capable, making daily connection through spiritual disciplines essential."[10] These healthy pastors acknowledge their God-dependence and discover that spiritual disciplines bring new life to their daily walk with God.

Just as solitude makes space for God, our physical environment can create space and foster a receptive spirit in us. You might want to find a comfortable place when you can settle for a while in silence, a place with minimal distractions. Some people find the light of a candle, soft instrumental music, or the gentle sounds of a water fountain soothe their emotions and engage their senses for worship.

One couple Keith and I know recently bought their first house—definitely a fixer-upper. We attended a party at their home, and they eagerly gave us a tour, proud to show us all their remodeling work. We came to a room at the back of the house and the wife quietly said, "This is our prayer room." Several beautiful framed photos adorned the walls—mountains and ocean scenes. A guitar rested against the wall. On a small table, a worn Bible rested next to a large white candle. The only other furniture in the room was a large overstuffed chair. The room whispered *peace*. This young couple, both serving in full-time ministry roles, had created a sacred space, an oasis for nurturing their spiritual lives. Perhaps you don't have an extra room to dedicate especially for prayer. You can still do small things to your environment to prompt you throughout the day to turn your mind God-ward.

Companions for the Journey

Our local fitness club seems to understand the value of peer support and accountability. They recently offered a two-for-one Buddy Special. People are more likely to engage in the discipline of a workout if a friend commits to do so with them or if they attend a class with several others to "share their pain."

When I attended seminary, I was married and both our children were in elementary school. The children and I did homework together in the evenings. My family supported me 100 percent in my educational preparation for ministry, and I am not sure if I could have made it without their encouragement and practical support.

I also discovered the value of the buddy system for my spiritual health. I had two friends who met with me once a week for prayer. They too were wives and mothers and they understood many of the pressures I faced. We prayed for each other. They knew when I faced exams and major deadlines. They also held me accountable to keep my eyes fixed on God in the midst of my busyness.

We never outgrow the need for a prayer partner. Many people have found great benefit in meeting regularly with a spiritual director, someone who guides them in their spiritual formation. No one is too spiritually mature to benefit from praying with another person or a small group. Even if you meet once a month or if your connection is never face-to-face but via e-mail and telephone, reach out and ask someone else to partner with you in prayer. Allow one or a few spiritual companions to participate with you in spiritual formation.

We have looked at two of the three foundational building blocks for spiritual well-being: balanced nutrition and regular exercise. God also has ordained the third building block: adequate rest. In the next chapter, we will explore what it means for us to experience a sabbath rest.

Assessment Journal

1. Choose one new spiritual discipline to practice daily for the next week. At the end of the week, consider the impact of that discipline and determine how you might make it a part of your ongoing spiritual formation patterns.
2. What might you do to create sacred space in your home?
3. What might you do to create sacred space in your office?

10

Sabbath

Rest for Your Soul

When I was growing up, our family often went out for Sunday dinner with friends after the morning church service. One of our favorite places was the Harvest House cafeteria at the local shopping mall. When we first started going there, the cafeteria was the only business open on Sundays. After we ate, we would stroll through the mall, looking at displays in shadowy windows and hearing our voices echo in the open spaces.

Then one Sunday at the mall we saw huge posters announcing that soon the rest of the mall would be open for business from 2:00 to 6:00 PM on Sunday afternoons. The women in our group greeted the news with excitement. Now they could shop after Sunday dinner. "It's about time they opened," my mother said. "I've never understood why people make such a big deal about shopping on Sundays." Mom's memories of Sundays as a child had caused her to vow not to repeat them when she had children of her own.

My mother was an only child, adopted by my grandparents when they were well into their thirties. Sabbath was a day for quiet. Following Sunday school and church, the family returned home for dinner and rest. Mom, a self-professed tomboy, was only permitted to sit inside the house and read her Sunday school papers or her Bible. It must have seemed like torture to her! The only thing she had to look forward to was a return to church for the evening service, which was conducted in Swedish, the native tongue of many adults in that immigrant community. My mother promised herself that once she was on her own, she would do things differently. And she did.

We went to church every Sunday. By the time I was born, the services were all in English. But other than attending services, our Sundays didn't look much different from the rest of the week. They were just one more day to catch up on things we needed to get done before school started again on Monday. Having the businesses open on Sunday afternoon would make it easier for us to run our errands.

"Remember the Sabbath day by keeping it holy. Six days you shall labor and do all your work, but the seventh day is a sabbath to the LORD your God. On it you shall not do any work, neither you, nor your son or daughter, nor your male or female servant, nor your animals, nor any foreigner residing in your towns. For in six days the LORD made the heavens and the earth, the sea, and all that is in them, but he rested on the seventh day. Therefore the LORD blessed the Sabbath day and made it holy" (Ex. 20:8-11).

Commandment four. I had learned all ten of them and my mother was very proud of my recitation. She believed that we should obey them—all except for number four. It was so outdated! Certainly, God didn't want us to sit around and be bored like she had been as a child. So my mother taught me to break God's commandment.

My grandparents had accepted a view of sabbath similar to that of the Pharisees. Sabbath practices were all about the shalt-nots, a long list of things to avoid. They got caught up in defining what it means to not do any work and to keep the day holy. Jesus challenged the rigid legalism of the Pharisees by healing on the sabbath. They called his miracles work; he called them freeing the captives from the infirmities that trapped them. Jesus said, "The Sabbath was made for people, not people for the Sabbath" (Mark 2:27). With their focus on rules and self-denial, the Pharisees (and my grandparents) missed the true freedom and meaning of sabbath. Sabbath was made for people. The fourth commandment is an invitation to come and rest, to find renewal and true refreshment.

Lynn Baab, in her book, *Sabbath Keeping*, defines sabbath as a "weekly day of rest and worship. A day to cease working and relax in God's care for us. A day to stop the things that occupy our workdays and participate in activities that nurture peace, worship, relationships, celebration and thankfulness."[1] Eugene Peterson refers to sabbath as God's gift given to resolve the competition between people and God for our attention. Perhaps to understand God's intention for the sabbath, we should look at the origins of sabbath practice.

Origins

We have already seen that God commanded a weekly sabbath when he gave Moses the law on Mount Sinai. Later, in Exodus 31:17, God indicated that refraining from work on the sabbath would be a sign of the covenant between God and Israel for the rest of the world to see Israel's commitment to God.

In Leviticus 25:1-5 God commanded the sabbatical year. Every seventh year the people were to allow the fields to lie fallow, to rest. After every seventh sabbatical year, (every fifty years) they were to celebrate Jubilee. The people of Israel did not do this.

In his book *Time Bomb in the Church*, Daniel Spaite traced the timeline from 1051 BC when Saul was king, until 606 when Judah was exiled—445 years, seventy sabbatical years, missed.[2] That is exactly how many years they spent in captivity. In 2 Chronicles 36:20-21 the writer reports that Nebuchadnezzar "carried into exile to Babylon the remnant, who escaped from the sword, and they became servants to him and his successors until the kingdom of Persia came to power. The land enjoyed its sabbath rests; all the time of its desolation it rested, until the seventy years were completed in fulfillment of the word of the LORD spoken by Jeremiah."

The same God who created the earth and commanded the sabbatical years and Jubilee created our bodies and commanded a weekly sabbath for us. If we ignore God's command, our bodies, like the land of Israel, will exact the time from us at some point. The person who refuses to take a God-ordained rest often ends up being forced to rest due to an injury or illness. God invites us to sabbath rest.

Pastors are often the worst offenders when it comes to breaking the sabbath commandment. I have had pastors tell me, "As long as I'm serving God, God will take care of me. I don't need to rest. I have important work to do." Nowhere in Scripture does God exempt the priests from sabbath observance. God invites us *all* to sabbath rest.

The Jews observe sabbath from sundown to sundown. They start their sabbath with rest from labor, which illustrates the priority of rest to the sabbath. Ray Anderson, in *The Shape of Practical Theology*, maintains that burnout among pastors is the result of a faulty theology related to sabbath. He wrote: "A theology allowing no 'sabbath rest' for the one who does the work of ministry is a theology of the curse, not a theology of the cross. A healthy theology contains healing for the healer and freedom for the fighter of God's battles."[3] Sabbath is a gift from God.

Sabbath Is a Break

The word *holy* means set aside for a special purpose or withdrawn from common employment and dedicated to God. To set aside a day for a special purpose suggests a break in weekly patterns. To withdraw from common employment means that sabbath should be an uncommon day in many dimensions.

Sabbath is a break from routine, a change of pace. Eugene Peterson, in *Working the Angles*, says that sabbath provides "Uncluttered time and space to distance ourselves from the frenzy of our own activities so we can see what God has been and is doing."[4] In the midst of your busyness and achieving, God calls you to rest, to lay aside your to-do lists and let the sabbath be different than the rest of your days. If your week is filled with e-mails and telephone calls, turn both machines off for the day. If your frantic schedule has you traveling all week, a sabbath at home will provide much-needed rest. If you spend your week cooped up in an office, a sabbath walk in the woods or an afternoon at the park playing with the kids may be just the space you need.

Wayne Muller, author of *Sabbath: Finding Rest, Renewal, and Delight in Our Busy Lives*, writes that sabbath should not be focused on legalism and prohibition. For Muller, the sabbath means "the space and time created to say yes to sacred spirituality, sensuality, sexuality, prayer, rest, song, delight. It is not about legalism and legislation, but about joy and the things that grow only in time."[5] The break in our routine allows us to delight ourselves in the things so often crowded out of our schedules. God promised joy to those who honor the sabbath: "If you call the Sabbath a delight and the LORD's holy day honorable, . . . then you will find your joy in the LORD" (Isa. 58:13-14).

Sabbath is a break from expectations and productivity. You don't need to accomplish anything in the true sabbath. We have become so conditioned to believe that unproductive time is wasted time. What things have you put off doing because you had more pressing deadlines? When was the last time you read a book just for fun? How long has it been since you turned off the alarm clock and slept in? Do you love to putter in the garden, but rarely find time for it? These things and many others may be ideal sabbath practices for you if you find them to be a source of refreshment.

In Deuteronomy 5, Moses repeated the Ten Commandments for the people of Israel. When he got to number four, the sabbath commandment, he added, "Remember that you were slaves in Egypt and that the LORD your God brought you out of there with a mighty hand and an outstretched arm. Therefore the LORD your God has commanded you to observe the Sabbath day" (Deut. 5:15). Eugene Peterson points out that the Israelites worked seven days a week while they were slaves in Egypt. "Never a day off. The consequence: they were no longer considered persons but slaves. Hands. Work units. Not persons created in the image of God but equipment for making bricks and building pyramids. Humanity was defaced."[6] When we become such slaves to accomplishment that we cannot break from it for at least a day, we become less than human.

Sabbath is a break from competition. For one day, we lay aside the pressure to be number one, to be better than anyone else. Competition pervades our society and the church and pushes us to try a little harder, give a little more to strive for the best. For the sabbath, lay aside the need to win and be content to participate in life. Choose not to engage in those activities that require competition. For example, I love to quilt. A restful sabbath might find me at my quilting frame, stitching a quilt for my grandson. While I work, I think of him and pray for him. I enjoy envisioning this quilt keeping him warm at night in the future. This labor of love truly brings me sabbath rest. If, however, I was quilting a project to enter into the state fair contest, my focus would be different. Every stitch would have to be perfect. As I worked, I would envision the quilt hanging on the wall with a blue ribbon and sense my pride in my accomplishment. I would push myself to be the best. There is not much sabbath rest in that scenario.

Sabbath is a break from consumerism. We spend so much time during the week thinking about making money, paying bills, and acquiring things we really need as well as those we just want. Our consumer society provides us with so many choices and upgrades that we can easily get sucked into the cycle of always wanting more. We want the newest gadget, the latest technology. God calls us to a life of simplicity. Especially on the sabbath, resolve to take the time to appreciate what you do have and refrain from the hectic grasping for more. Sabbath is a good time to ask, "Do I really need that?" and discern what is really important.

Sabbath is a break from being in control. This may be the hardest thing for pastors to lay down. So many people depend on us. We carry heavy loads of responsibility that creates for us the illusion that we have control. Parents leaving their baby alone with a sitter for the first time often worry, what if the baby gets sick? What if she gets hurt? What if he cries? Will the sitter know how to handle it? In reality, babies get sick or hurt even when the parents are home. Parents cannot always prevent or control that any more than a sitter could. In the event that a problem arises, the babysitter probably can handle it or the parents would not have trusted the sitter in the first place; they have an emergency number to reach the parents as a last resort. The child will get along just fine without the parents for the evening.

In essence, you (the pastor) are leaving your child (the church) for the day when you take a sabbath. Are they grown up enough to take care of themselves? Can the world survive if you step off the merry-go-round for a day and aren't around to run things? The real, underlying question is "Can you trust God to take care of things in your absence?"

Sabbath Brings Refreshment

Jesus invites the weary and burdened to come to him and rest (Matt. 11:28). Sabbath allows us the space to commune with God and find rest in that fellowship.

David wrote, "Truly my soul finds rest in God; my salvation comes from him. Truly he is my rock and my salvation; he is my fortress, I will never be shaken" (Ps. 62:1-2). The security David found in God was like resting safely behind the walls of a strong fortress.

We all need refreshment, but what refreshes you may be different from what refreshes me. We each need to design sabbath practices that meet our individual needs for refreshment. I asked a group of pastors to tell me the first words that came to their minds when they thought of sabbath. Several mentioned food: feasts and potlucks. Others mentioned naps or physical rest. One said time alone and another listed fellowship and family. One pastor painted a full word picture of himself sitting alongside a mountain stream, fishing pole in one hand, thermos of coffee in the other. That was his weekly sabbath; he truly understood what he needed for refreshment and he headed for the hills every week.

You may not be as clear about what refreshes you. It may have been so long since you took a sabbath that you don't know what you need. Choose something that will provide a break from your routine and try it out for a few weeks. You may need to try several different things until you discover sabbath patterns that fit you. Let's consider several aspects of sabbath renewal.

Sabbath Brings Renewal

The word *renewal* suggests making things that have become old and familiar new again. Sabbath brings social renewal. A sabbath day provides time for us to renew our relationships with others, building new connections and new memories. In most Jewish homes, sabbath begins with the sabbath meal shared with family and friends. How many times have you said to someone, "We really should get together more often" after an evening of good food and conversation? Sabbath provides an excellent opportunity to do just that, to relax with good friends, enjoying relationships that are mutually nurturing.

Sabbath also provides time to reconnect with your spouse. Often in the course of weekly schedules at church and children's school activities, ministry couples begin to feel like two ships that pass in the night or strangers who just happen to share a bed. Develop a sabbath ritual together. Some couples have declared sabbath a day for no alarm clock and a leisurely breakfast together. Others take long walks or visit museums together. Wayne Muller reports that "among the many Sabbath practitioners who have shared their stories with me, one of the more popular Sabbath activities is making love. Indeed, the Talmud tractate on marriage contracts states that the righteous couple should make love every Friday night."[7] Although a rigid weekly rule for lovemaking might seem unromantic and may even be counterproductive, the primary message is that sabbath provides time for intimacy and renewal of relationship.

Sabbath brings spiritual renewal. Eugene Peterson calls this "Quieting the internal noise so we hear the still small voice of our Lord. Removing the distractions of pride so we discern the presence of Christ."[8] Sabbath provides extended time to practice any of the spiritual disciplines. The Jewish sabbath often includes lighting candles and singing spiritual songs and concludes with a special prayer of blessing for each child in the family. You may decide, as many pastors do, that Sunday cannot be a true day of rest for you and you may choose another day of the week for your personal sabbath. Whatever day you choose, plan to include a deliberate time of worship, a time when you focus your full attention on God in awe and reverence.

Sabbath also brings physical renewal. For most of us that means, in part, catching up on sleep from which we have deprived ourselves throughout the week. It may mean allowing yourself to follow your body's urging and take a nap when you feel drowsy at midday. But physical renewal also involves activity and stimulation of all of your senses in some break from routine. This may mean taking walks, alone or with family or friends; playing catch with the kids; or having a snowball fight. Satisfying your hunger for beauty and for good scents, good food, and beautiful sounds will renew you physically. Think of the imagery of Psalm 23. David says that

God restores his soul. David's language reveals God ministering to him in a very physical, sensate way: green pastures, quiet waters, a table (feast), and soothing oil. Allow God to restore your soul on the sabbath as you find physical renewal.

Common Misunderstandings about Sabbath

Many people resist taking sabbath because they think it is selfish. Or perhaps they tried to take a sabbath and someone else accused them of being lazy. Sabbath keeping is obedience to God's plan and commandment. If that is not enough reason, sabbath keeping is essential self-care for the pastor. Parker Palmer wrote, "By surviving passages of doubt and depression on the vocational journey, I have become clear about at least one thing: self-care is never a selfish act—it is simply good stewardship of the only gift I have, the gift I was put on earth to offer others."[9]

Sabbath is *not* a sign of weakness. Some people will say, "I don't need a rest. I have lots of energy; I'm a Type A person. Sabbath is only for sissies." God not only commanded the sabbath but also took the very first sabbath. God didn't *need* to take a break; but God chose to establish a rhythm of work and sabbath. Jesus also followed the general sabbath practices of his day, in spite of his few recorded run-ins with the Pharisees.

Sabbath is not simply a day off. While time away from work is important, Eugene Peterson calls the day off a secularized sabbath. "The motivation is utilitarian: the day off is at the service of the six working days. The purpose is to restore strength, increase motivation, reward effort, and keep performance incentives high."[10] The distinction between "day off" and "sabbath" is not merely one of semantics. Peterson calls it a sign of abandoned pastoral identity. A day off conjures images of chores and simply doing whatever needs to be done, substituting home pressures for church pressures—hardly a picture of renewal. Sabbath implies a deliberately restful day focused on God and filled with just the right amount of people and activities to refresh you and restore your soul.

In her book *Keeping the Sabbath Wholly: Ceasing, Resting, Embracing, Feasting*, Marva Dawn wrote about the importance of keeping sabbath: "When we order our lives around the focus of our relationship with God by letting our Sabbath day be the highlight of our week, toward which everything moves and from which everything comes, then the security of God's presence on that day will pervade the week."[11] If you remember the sabbath and keep it holy, you will find new appreciation for this gift from God. Respond to God's invitation to sabbath rest. The remainder of your life and ministry will be transformed and enriched as well.

Assessment Journal

1. What keeps you from honoring a sabbath day?
2. Do you lose your sense of value when you are not working?
3. Do you avoid quiet time to avoid yourself?
   - Can you sit quietly and reflect on your day or do you find yourself uncomfortable with silence and solitude?
   - Find a comfortable chair and sit in a relaxed position. Ask yourself, "How did I see God in my life today?" You may want to simply meditate or you may prefer to write your thoughts in a journal. If you have trouble remaining in your chair, you may be avoiding self-reflection.
4. Do you avoid sabbath time with your family?
   - Do you share a meal together with your family, lingering at the table in conversation?
   - Although we all need time alone (see question 3), we are also called to healthy relationships. Sometimes we seek

solitude to avoid the intimacy and risk of relationship. How is the balance between alone time and with-others time in your life?

5. What misconceptions have you held about sabbath in the past?

6. Establish short-term and long-term goals for yourself about sabbath keeping. What practices will you start building immediately? What do you want to work toward? If you can't find a full day each week, resolve to start with a half-day sabbath or an evening each week. You may find it so refreshing that you will start building your whole weekly calendar around your sabbath, creating space for the full day that you really need.

11

Extended Sabbath Rest

I have always loved retreats. When I was in sixth grade I couldn't wait for the next year when I would be old enough to join the youth group and go on the annual retreat like my big brother. I wasn't even sure what happened at retreats, but I knew it would be special. Three days and two nights away from home had to be special, and the teens always came home with new energy and lots of fun stories.

I can't count how many retreats I have been to since I reached seventh grade. I have gone to retreats for teens, women, college students, singles, church choir, pastors and spouses, couples, church boards, student leadership groups, pastoral staff, and faculty. Every one had a unique focus and purpose. They all share one thing in common: an extended time away from the daily routine of home. Some things just can't happen amid the daily-ness of life; retreats provide extended times to focus on those things. For some, the goal is fun, rest, and relaxation. Other retreats have a business focus. All retreats offer opportunity for building relationships through extended time together. Even a solitary spiritual retreat includes a focus on building your relationship with God.

On occasion, we all need extended time away. No matter how faithfully we follow sabbath practices, there comes a time when we feel the need for a break to do those things that just can't happen in the midst of day-to-day schedules. Many pastors are discovering the benefit of extended sabbath rest in the form of retreats and sabbaticals.

Retreats

Amber* sat on the edge of her seat in my office. Her hands fidgeted with her water bottle as she said, "I just feel so jumpy. I'm tired and I can't focus real well. I've just been out of sorts with people. Then I realized the other day that it's been ages since I've been up to the convent, so I scheduled a weekend there. I'm hoping that helps me get back on track." The convent to which she referred is in a city nearby. The sisters manage a retreat center and offer guided and silent retreats and spiritual direction.

The next time I saw Amber she looked like a different person. She sat back in the chair with her hands resting in her lap and said, "It was so good to spend time alone with God. Just two days in God's presence and I feel so much more at peace." As a full-time seminary student also holding down a full-time job, Amber fit her spiritual disciplines in the cracks in her schedule. These practices carried her in the short term, but she needed the occasional time away with God to sustain her over the long haul. She tried to take a two-day retreat each month to pray and bathe her spirit in the silence.

Kathy* was the pastor of a church on the edge of the city. This small congregation was excited about their new pastor and invited family, friends, and coworkers to visit their church. The congregation grew and Pastor Kathy found herself overwhelmed. As we visited one day, she told me how busy she was with meetings, church property and finance issues, new believers' classes, and planning vacation Bible school. "This will be the first VBS in the church's history," she said proudly. "With all the new families coming, we have lots of kids now." Then she frowned, "With all the new families, I also have a lot more people wanting my time. Some of their lives are such a mess! It's all I can do to find time to prepare my sermon each week." I asked when she had taken her last sabbath and she assured me that Thursday was her day. Every week, she never missed sabbath. But the other six days of the week she was running nonstop.

One of the habits that Pastor Kathy began to develop was to plan a quarterly retreat for herself and two lay people who were volunteer staff at the church. Every thirteen weeks she would head out of town on Thursday to a retreat center in the nearby countryside. She spent Thursday and Friday alone with God, reading Scripture, praying and listening, reflecting on God's call in her life, and soaking in the scenic beauty around her. She would journal her thoughts and by Friday afternoon, she began sketching out a preaching schedule for the next thirteen weeks. This time alone helped Pastor Kathy reorient herself to what she saw as essential and gain a greater sense of purpose in her daily ministry.

After work ended on Friday, the lay volunteer staff joined her. Together they would spend Friday evening in worship and prayer. Saturday morning they dreamed together and planned six months or more in advance for the various ministries of the church. The extended time allowed them to reorient themselves, individually and as a team, and focus on God. Then they were ready to hear God's voice and discern direction for their ongoing work in the church.

The model that Pastor Kathy and the church's volunteer staff developed could be used by any pastor. You can adapt it in any way that fits you, your personal spiritual practices, and the needs of your church. The length of time, schedule (or lack thereof), and location will vary according to your unique situation. The essential element remains constant: time set aside, away from the work-day environment and its distractions, to focus on your relationship with God and your service to God.

When I was in high school my older brother came home from college one weekend for a visit. At dinner I told him about the upcoming teen retreat and how much I was looking forward to it. With all of his new-found collegiate wisdom, he asked, "Why do they call it a retreat? They really ought to call it an 'advance' if it's supposed to help you move forward. 'Retreat' sounds like you're running away." At the time I dismissed him as a smart aleck, but his words have stayed with me. They carry an element of truth. God calls us to retreat from the busyness of life for extended time with him. We can use that time in many ways. As pastors we hunger for that time for prayer, vision development, and planning. The time that we spend in retreat enables us to advance when we return to our place of ministry as renewed leaders.

Sabbaticals

In Leviticus 25:1-7 God commanded the people of Israel to honor a sabbatical year in addition to the weekly sabbath. Every seventh year they were to allow the fields to rest, neither planting nor harvesting. In modern times, farmers have discovered the value of giving fields a year of rest and of rotating crops grown in a given field to allow the nutrients in the soil to replenish in order to later grow healthier and stronger crops. For the Israelites, the pattern of planting and harvesting for six years and resting for one year established a sabbatical rhythm.

For many years, professors at colleges and universities have known the rhythm of sabbatical. Typically, after seven years of full-time teaching, a professor may apply for a period of time away from teaching and administrative responsibilities to focus on travel, research, and writing. Sabbatical plans vary according to the nature of the institution and the faculty member's field of expertise. Some who teach in scientific or technical fields may spend their sabbatical time in a laboratory, learning updated techniques or conducting experiments. An artist or writer might spend a significant part of the sabbatical leave creating new works or trying out a new art medium or writing genre. Professors in all subject areas may travel to observe the work of others in their field or to develop collaborative projects with colleagues and other institutions.

Regardless of the individual's area of expertise, faculty sabbaticals appear to have three general expectations. First, the sabbatical provides respite from the regular teaching load (and all the preparation, grading, and student advising that go along with it) and from other institutional expectations (including committee work and participation in special events). Second, the person on sabbatical will put that set-aside time to good use in retooling for teaching. He or she may spend time reading those things that have piled up in the busyness of daily teaching and catch up on the latest developments in the field. Catching up may include travel, new experiences, and the like. Third, out of the new learning and growth that occurs in the freed-up time to study and reflect will emerge a product of some sort. In much of the academic world, the expected product of a sabbatical is a book or a number of articles written. The product may also be the development of a new course or program or the completion of specialized continuing education. The three expectations might be summed up as respite, retooling, and results.

After twenty years of teaching in university and seminary settings, I see the wisdom of sabbatical rhythm. Most professors carry full loads with classes, student contact, committees, and various administrative tasks. When the professor teaches the same course every year, it becomes easy to rely on the old lecture notes and repeat the same things year after year. We can get into ruts, although we might euphemistically call them "comfortable routines." Simply put, sabbatical provides the time and impetus to reflect on what we do, why we do it, and how we might do it better in the future.

Our day-to-day work is enhanced by our special time apart and we gain new perspective.

The same results are possible for pastors who develop a sabbatical rhythm. For years, common wisdom has held that longer tenure in a given congregation enhances the productivity and effectiveness of pastoral ministry. As relationships grow over time, trust develops between people and pastor, whereas rapid clergy turnover inhibits relationship building. Given time together, minister and parishioners learn each other's strengths and build working systems to enhance those gifts. However, Roy Oswald, formerly a senior consultant with the Alban Institute, cited a Gap Theory that somewhere between seven and ten years into a pastor's ministry in a congregation, people begin to wonder if their pastor is giving them sufficient corporate leadership.[1] They may question whether this person with whom they have become so familiar has the right stuff to take them the next step into the future. Often in this same time period, the pastor may begin to wonder if the congregation has what it takes to move into the future. Other pastures may look greener. A gap develops between pastor and people.

Experts who study congregations suggest that rather than a new pastor, the best solution to this developing gap is a renewed pastor. They propose clergy sabbaticals as a means of renewal for both pastor and congregation that will enhance ministry continuity. Apparently a number of pastors agree with this position. In 2001, Duke Divinity School surveyed Catholic and Protestant clergy and 30 percent reported having taken a sabbatical. Rabbi David Stern, senior rabbi of Temple Emanu-El in Dallas, Texas, himself the beneficiary of a sabbatical leave, reports many rabbis seeking his advice on arranging for their own sabbaticals as well.[2] Clearly, interest and participation in this form of ministry renewal is growing. A recent Internet search using the key words "clergy sabbaticals" produced over ten thousand sources.

The experts who recommend sabbatical rhythm for clergy and the pastors who have written about their sabbatical experience offer principles and specific suggestions that may guide you as you consider the role of sabbatical in your ministry.

Sabbatical may not be the best answer for every pastor. Melissa Bane Sevier, in her book on pastoral sabbaticals, warns that "sabbatical is not for clergy who are burned out; however, it may keep us from becoming burned out by giving us renewal in spirit, vision, and call."[3] The pastor who is burned out needs to seek counseling and work to get emotionally healthy before he or she could even benefit from the self-directed process of a sabbatical. Sevier also suggests that a pastor in the midst of serious marital conflict or family difficulties should seek immediate help, but warns against viewing sabbatical as a solution to personal problems. Also a sabbatical is not the time for a pastor to decide whether or not to stay at a given charge. The ideal candidate for sabbatical is the pastor who is fundamentally healthy, yet recognizes the need for new vision and energy in order to continue in vital ministry in her or his current place of service.

To make the most of sabbatical for both the pastor and the congregation requires advanced planning and good communication. This means you don't want to wait until you feel the need for sabbatical, because you may not have enough time to prepare well before you burn out. Establish a sabbatical rhythm, knowing that you are human and you will need that refreshment; then begin planning for it. You need to plan for your time and work with the congregation to plan for its time while you are away.

Your plan requires thought. The sabbatical is not intended as simply an extended vacation. Sabbatical provides release from the daily demands of ministry to allow a time for rest and renewal, not disengagement and aimlessness. Since 1998, the Lilly Endowment has offered grants for clergy sabbaticals through their Clergy Renewal Program.[4] They state that "Renewal periods are not vacations, but times for intentional exploration and reflection, for drinking again from God's life-giving waters, for regaining enthusiasm and creativity for ministry."[5] With that caveat, we will consider what a sabbatical plan might include, working with the three basic expectations mentioned above: respite, retooling, and results.

Resting

Resting is an essential element of sabbatical. However, resting means far more than napping. If you have not already established a consistent sabbath pattern, sabbatical time may be the ideal opportunity to set up a deliberate weekly sabbath habit that you will commit to continue after you return to ministry responsibilities. Resting implies making space for reflection. Many pastors (and professors) find that when they first step away from their workload, they have to fight the habitual urge to pick up the phone or send an e-mail. After a while, though, the reality of the break sets in and they begin to relax. At this point, the pastor often experiences physical exhaustion and may be surprised at the decompression time needed. Don't resist your body's needs. Several days of unscheduled time to read, pray, reflect, and sleep according to the body's demands may suffice to restore physical energy. Use the sabbatical period to reestablish healthy sleep patterns and commit to carrying those restful patterns over into postsabbatical life.

A change of pace—doing things out of the ordinary pattern—in itself is refreshing. During sabbatical, your pace may change quantitatively; you need to resist the temptation to simply substitute a new busyness for your normal daily routine. Don't add new things just to fill up the time. Your pace will also change qualitatively; what you devote time to will change. Say no to internal pressure to achieve and accomplish "something of value." Following her sabbatical, Rev. Terry Rae Anderson, pastor of Family of Grace Lutheran Church, Auburn, Washington, wrote, "Rest included time to sit and watch rain drops on the window and to revel in sunshine that warmed the earth and beckoned spring flowers to bloom. In quiet moments all to myself, I contemplated the intersection of my reading and my life."[6] In ministry more than in any other occupation, *who you are* is closely tied to *what you do*. During sabbatical, time and energy focus on *being* more than on *doing*. The Rev. Dr. Vanessa Allen-Brown, recipient of a Clergy Renewal Program grant, offered this advice for pastors considering a sabbatical: "Dream, dream, dream . . . I invite them to seek out the things that make their heart sing and dance. I invite them to reconnect with their calling to ministry and to God's people."[7]

Retooling

Retooling may be the heart of the sabbatical plan. What new things do you want to experience, to learn in this time? What will make your heart sing? Retooling may mean gaining new skills for ministry, adding new tools to your ministry toolbox. Sometimes, observing new practices through "site visits to churches and conversations with church leaders helps the pastor to find out what is working for others and what might be helpful in his/her own church."[8]

Renewal may also come from gaining skills, experience, or knowledge in a wide variety of areas. The topic of exploration may not seem directly related to ministry. However, whatever makes the pastor a deeper, healthier, more vibrant individual will impact the pastor's ministry as well. Recent recipients of the National Clergy Renewal Program awards typify the wide variety of sabbatical experiences that can enrich the life and future ministry of a minister. Some plan to travel outside the country to visit mission schools, churches, or museums; others to study a foreign language or tour significant sites in their denominational history. One anticipates an audience with Pope Benedict XVI in Rome. One will visit urban churches in London; another will talk with rural pastors throughout the midwestern United States. Past recipients have studied theater and the visual arts and have taken music lessons. In your plan, take into account your gifts, interests, and passions.

Sabbatical offers an opportunity for spiritual retooling as well. You might consider taking an extended spiritual retreat or working with a spiritual director to focus intentionally on deepening your relationship with God. Sabbatical provides space for you to spend time with God for the sheer pleasure of growing closer to God, without any thought of how you might translate your experience into words that you will use for a lesson or sermon.

One other realm of sabbatical retooling is social renewal. Some pastors choose to use part of their sabbatical time visiting with extended family or renewing connections with old friends in distant places. Rev. Jay Alan Hobbs, rector of the Episcopal Church of the Good Shepherd in Dallas, traveled with his wife to visit all of their former places of ministry and spent time with children and grandchildren together at a beach in Florida.[9]

Results

Results will also be part of the plan, but we cannot always predict some outcomes. Just as the options for renewal and retooling seem endless, so, too, the results of sabbatical are many and varied. Some pastors will return to their ministry setting with a tangible product of the sabbatical—a book, article, or creative piece such as a painting or song. Others may develop slide shows or lesson series out of what they learned and saw during their sabbatical. But whether or not there is a tangible product depends on the original plan and is actually of secondary importance. The most important result of the sabbatical is the renewal that occurs in the pastor. No one returns from a sabbatical experience the same person he or she was before; a qualitative change has taken place.

Rev. Vincent Rush, pastor of Saint Hugh of Lincoln Roman Catholic Church, Huntington Station, New York, reported that his sabbatical experience heightened his self-awareness and enabled him to become more self-differentiated and emotionally healthy.[10] When he returned to parish ministry, his relationships in the church improved accordingly. While on her sabbatical, Rev. Dr. Vanessa Allen-Brown traveled. She did not study preaching methods. Yet when she returned, she reported that her sermons "were more vibrant, bold, and challenging."[11] She had experienced a new vibrancy that extended into her preaching ministry. She returned to her congregation a *renewed* pastor.

So you are convinced you need to establish a sabbatical rhythm. Ideas and dreams take shape in your mind. But what about your church? How can you help them see that sabbatical for you will be good for them, too? Melissa Bane Sevier says that there are three hot button questions for the church: "Will the pastor return?" "Where will the money come from?" and "How will the congregation manage?" Clear, open communication on these issues can bring pastor and people together in a plan for growth for all. Framing the sabbatical as a shared process may facilitate the conversation.

Some churches have good reason to fear the pastor will leave following a sabbatical. They have seen it happen or know of a place where the pastor used a church-supported leave to explore another position. Others may have this fear because of confusion over the idea of sabbatical. Anything you can do to clarify the purpose of sabbatical may help assuage those fears. You might invite a judicatory official to meet with the congregation and explain the purpose and process of sabbatical to members and discuss concerns with them. One or two other pastors who have taken a sabbatical and returned to their congregations refreshed could come and share their stories. Sevier suggests that if fears persist, the pastor might offer written assurance of intent to return for at least a year after the sabbatical. Most educational institutions have such return expectations written into their faculty handbook policy on sabbaticals.

Funding for sabbatical may come from a variety of sources. The Lilly Endowment Clergy Renewal Program has already been mentioned. In 2006, they funded sabbaticals for 127 pastors with grants of up to $45,000 each. The Louisville Institute has a Sabbatical Grant for Pastoral Leaders program. Some denominationally based programs are available. The potential amount of funding available will determine the activities of the sabbatical plan, but minimal funding need not prevent sabbatical—it should only shape the budget. Some churches set aside money every year so that in the seventh year of the sabbatical rhythm adequate funds will be available to support the sabbatical program. Many retreat centers and campgrounds have spaces designated and available for clergy at no or low cost.[12] Investigate all possible sources of funding as you begin your sabbatical planning.

The third concern mentioned by Sevier is perhaps the easiest to answer. To the question, "How will we get along without our pastor?" the short answer is "Just fine." The long version of the answer is that a pastor's sabbatical provides opportunity for the congregation to stretch, to share responsibility for their church, and to grow.

When our children were little, Keith and I received some excellent advice from a friend: if we went out without the kids, we should plan something special for them to look forward to at home so they wouldn't feel left out. We would get their favorite babysitter (Jenniffer), let them choose their dinner (usually macaroni and cheese with hot dogs), and let them plan a fun evening (baking cookies, going to the park, or a special video were the favorites). They rarely complained about being left behind.

The congregation with their own sabbatical plan needn't feel abandoned. A special interim speaker may come for the entire time and offer a series of classes or sermons. If the substitute has different gifts from the pastor, the change can also be renewing for the parishioners. In other congregations, the lay people may choose to organize and divide up responsibilities among themselves. One such congregation, Community Christian Church in Kansas City, Missouri, established a Sabbatical Oversight Ad hoc

Review (SOAR) committee.[13] They invited two guest ministers to fill the pulpit in the pastor's absence and the SOAR committee, in conjunction with the church staff, assumed responsibility to ensure coverage in all areas of administration, pastoral care, and worship leadership. They even began their planning by sending a brochure and pastoral letter to the whole congregation.

The ideal response of the congregation when the pastor returns from sabbatical will be twofold: first, "Although we missed you, we did well while you were gone," and second, "We're glad you're back; we now have a better idea of what you do all week long!"

Sabbatical rhythm benefits the pastor, restoring the soul (Ps. 23). Sabbatical rhythm also benefits the congregation, providing challenges, growth, and the blessing of a renewed pastor. The sabbatical provides space for the pastor to build his or her gifts, growing in self-awareness and fulfillment in ministry. The sabbatical creates space to spend time with God, strengthening the pastor's spiritual walk that in turn will enhance the pastor's future ministry and relationships.

Assessment Journal

1. When was the last time you took a retreat for prayer, visioning, and planning?
   • Where did you go? Have you already scheduled your next retreat?
   • If you have never taken a retreat before, where might you go and when?
2. If you have ever taken a sabbatical, reflect in your journal on your experience in light of the principles of rest, retooling, and results.
3. Does your congregation have a sabbatical policy in place for all pastoral staff?

- If your answer is yes, when will your next sabbatical be? Use your journal to begin thinking about your plan in terms of rest, retooling, and results.
- If your answer is no, does your denomination have a sabbatical policy that will support you as you approach your church leadership on this issue?

4. What do you need to do to initiate conversation about sabbatical with lay leaders?

5. Review your long-term goals from chapter 3. Which, if any, of these might guide your sabbatical planning?

12

Blessing

The LORD bless you
and keep you;
the LORD make his face shine on you
and be gracious to you;
the LORD turn his face toward you
and give you peace.

—Numbers 6:24-26

A couple of years ago, I had one of those "significant" birthdays. You know, the kind with a zero in the age. My husband asked me to choose my celebration. I knew I wanted my family with me that day. My children, their spouses, and my grandson all came to town for the weekend. For two hours, we invited just about everyone we know to drop by the house and share my favorite food: warm chocolate chip cookies (with the chips still melted!). Our friends, Ron and Sherry, served up hot cookies straight from the oven all afternoon. The house overflowed with people, conversation, hugs, and good smells.

What a joy it was for me to introduce my adult children and their spouses to our friends they had not yet met. So many people that I love, all in one place: family, colleagues from school, friends from church, students, long-time friends from churches where we served long ago. The entire day was a blessing to me.

My daughter created a Blessing Book for me in honor of the day. On the front page she put my first grade school portrait and on the next page came a baby picture and an old birth announcement. The rest of this beautiful book is filled with photos from the party and notes of benediction. Some of those notes were written at the party. Others came from friends and family literally around the world that could not be there to celebrate with us.

As I reflect on that day and why it blessed me so deeply, I believe it confirms what I have tried to say in this book. I am connected for life. I find vitality and purpose for each day in my relationships and I believe that relationships sustain me for the long haul, the full length of my life. My birthday celebration reflected all the relationships of my life.

My relationship with myself showed through because I was encouraged to celebrate *my* way. As an extravert, I wanted to spend the day with people, talking and hugging. We ate my favorite food and skipped the birthday cake with all the candles. The written notes confirmed my gifts and strengths as some shared how my friendship or teaching had impacted their lives. (No one mentioned growing edges on that day!) It was authentically my day.

My connection with people in the family, the church, and the community were also represented in those who took time to join the celebration or to send notes. Some had known our kids as toddlers. One woman who came had known my husband all his life. Many had walked with us and prayed with us through some very dark valleys.

My relationship with God permeated the day because I know that each of these people that I love is a gift from God. My heart overflowed that day with prayers of thanksgiving. Many conversations resonated along themes of faith, talk of recent retreats, Sunday school lessons, mission trips, and prayer support. I take the book out every once in a while and smile as I read the messages. Sometimes I shed a few tears of joy as I recall these people I love so much.

My prayer is that your Assessment Journal will in some way become for you a Blessing Book. I encourage you to go back and read once again your self-assessment and the goals that you prayerfully set out for yourself. Live with those pages until you are able to genuinely thank God for creating you uniquely. Commit those plans to God, allowing yourself to dare to envision God's future for you.

As you reread what you have written in your journal about relationships with others, (chapters 4 through 7) thank God for the people in your family, church, and community. Commit yourself to do what you need to do in order to strengthen those ties; these ties bring you life! Whom do you need to call today? What will you do this week to reach out and connect with others?

As you have read the final section (chapters 8 through 11), I hope you have already begun new practices that draw you nearer to God. I pray that you will experience the truth of the words of the hymn:

> There is a place of comfort sweet, Near to the heart of God;
> A place where we our Savior meet, Near to the heart of God.
> There is a place of full release, Near to the heart of God;
> A place where all is joy and peace, Near to the heart of God.[1]

Commit yourself to making and living out new plans to create space in your life to hear God speak his blessing to you.

The familiar words of blessing with which I began this chapter are the Priestly Blessing that God commanded Aaron to pronounce to bless the Israelites. But I didn't learn that blessing in church. I first learned these words in my public school. Our high school music director, a devout Christian, closed every choir concert with these words, set to music by Peter C. Lutkin. Any choir alumni in the audience were invited to come up onto the stage and sing, too, so we might have two- to three-hundred people raising their voices in benediction.

In my own voice and in my own words, I echo this ancient blessing to you:

The Lord bless you and keep you . . .
May you know the assurance of God's sustaining hand upon your life.
The Lord make his face shine on you and be gracious to you . . .
May you know and receive God's pardoning grace as God's very presence shines into your life.
The Lord turn his face toward you and give you peace . . .
God's entire being is given to bring about your salvation.
May you know God's peace that passes all understanding.
The Lord bless you as you build blessed connections in your life.
Amen.

Notes

Introduction

1. H. B. London Jr. and Neil Wiseman, *Pastors at Greater Risk* (Ventura, CA: Regal Books, 2003), 20.
2. Christina Maslach and S. E. Jackson, "The Measurement of Experienced Burnout," *Journal of Occupational Behavior* 2: 99-113.
3. Judith Schwanz, "A Model of Role Conflict, Role Ambiguity, and Personality Factors in Relation to Burnout in the Christian Ministry" (PhD diss., Portland State University, 1996).
4. In his book *Ministry Burnout*, John Sanford lists nine particular difficulties ministers face in their work: (1) the job is never finished, (2) they can't always see results, (3) the work is repetitive, (4) they deal with people's expectations, (5) they work with the same people year in and year out, (6) working with people in need drains energy, (7) many parishioners just want "strokes," not real spiritual food, (8) they must function in their persona much of the time, (9) they may become exhausted by failure.
5. For more on this issue, see Guy Greenfield, *The Wounded Minister: Healing from and Preventing Personal Attacks* (Grand Rapids, MI: Baker Books, 2001); Kenneth C. Haugk, *Antagonists in the Church: How to Identify and Deal with Destructive Conflict* (Minneapolis: Augsburg Publishing House, 1988);

Arthur Paul Boers, *Never Call Them Jerks: Healthy Responses to Difficult Behavior* (Herndon, VA: The Alban Institute, 1999); and G. Lloyd Rediger, *Clergy Killers: Guidance for Pastors and Congregations Under Attack* (Louisville, KY: Westminster/John Knox, 1997).

6. Daniel Spaite, *Time Bomb in the Church: Defusing Pastoral Burnout* (Kansas City, MO: Beacon Hill Press, 1999).

7. Ray Sherman Anderson, *The Shape of Practical Theology: Empowering Ministry with Theological Praxis* (Downers Grove, IL: InterVarsity Press, 2001).

8. Gary D. Kinnaman and Alfred H. Ells, *Leaders That Last: How Covenant Friendships Can Help Pastors Thrive* (Grand Rapids, MI: Baker Books, 2003).

9. Peter Salovey and John D. Mayer, "Emotional Intelligence," *Imagination, Cognition and Personality* 9 (1990): 185-211.

10. Daniel Goleman, *Emotional Intelligence: Why It Can Matter More Than IQ* (New York: Bantam Books, 1995).

11. Daniel Goleman, Richard Boyatzis, and Annie McKee, *Primal Leadership: Realizing the Power of Emotional Intelligence* (Boston: Harvard Business School Press, 2002).

12. Chad Johnson, "Emotional Intelligence: The Core of the Church Leader for Missional Living in the Emerging Culture" (DMin diss., George Fox Evangelical Seminary, 2005).

Chapter 1, Truly Authentic

1. Chad Johnson, "Emotional Intelligence," 64.

2. Gordon MacDonald, "Working with Your Emotional Type," *ChristianityTodayLibrary.com*, http://www.ctlibrary.com/6019. Originally in Gordon MacDonald, Maxie D. Dunnam, and Donald W. McCullough, *Mastering Personal Growth*, (Sisters, OR: Multnomah Publishers, 1992).

3. The Johari Window is available in multiple places, but one of the first published sources is Joseph Luft, *Group Processes: An Introduction to Group Dynamics* (Palo Alto, CA: Mayfield Publishing Co., 1963).

4. Henri J. M. Nouwen, *The Wounded Healer: Ministry in Contemporary Society* (New York: Doubleday Publishing, 1972).

5. Parker J. Palmer, *Let Your Life Speak: Listening for the Voice of Vocation* (San Francisco: Jossey-Bass, 2000), 49-50.

Chapter 2, Self-Assessment

1. Sanguine is one of four personality types proposed by the ancient Greek historian Hippocrates and made popular in the writings of both Tim LaHaye and Florence Littauer. The other three are choleric, melancholy, and phlegmatic. For more on this model, see Florence Littauer's Web site www.thepersonalities.com.

2. *Gifts Differing: Understanding Personality Type* by Isabel Briggs Myers (Palo Alto, CA: Davies-Black Publishing, 1995) and *Please Understand Me II* by David Keirsey (Del Mar, CA: Prometheus Nemesis Book Co., 1998) are classic resources. Consulting Psychologists Press (www.cpp.com) and the Center for Applications of Psychological Type (www.capt.org) offer certification training and other resource materials.

3. Roy M. Oswald and Otto Kroeger, *Personality Type and Religious Leadership* (Herndon, VA: The Alban Institute, 1988).

4. See www.capt.org for information on finding a certified administrator in your area or taking the inventory online.

5. For more information, see www.strengthsquest.com. The book *StrengthsQuest: Discover and Develop Your Strengths in Academics, Career, and Beyond* by Donald O. Clifton and Edward "Chip" Anderson (Washington, D.C.: The Gallup Organization, 2001-2004) comes with a computer access code so that the individual

can take the assessment online and receive a computer-generated report.

6. Corrine Ware, *Discover Your Spiritual Type: A Guide to Individual and Congregational Growth* (Herndon, VA: The Alban Institute, 1995).
7. Palmer, *Let Your Life Speak*, 79.

Chapter 3, Setting Your Direction

1. For more on asset-based planning for organizations, see Bob Sitze, *Not Trying Too Hard: New Basics for Sustainable Congregations* (Herndon, VA: The Alban Institute, 2001).
2. Lewis B. Smedes, *Shame and Grace: Healing the Shame We Don't Deserve* (San Francisco: HarperCollins, 1993).
3. Smedes's book *Shame and Grace* may be a place to start the healing process. Consult a trusted friend or counselor for assistance along your healing journey.

Chapter 4, Created for Relationship

1. Stephen Seamands, *Ministry in the Image of God: The Trinitarian Shape of Christian Service* (Downers Grove, IL: InterVarsity Press, 2005), 35.
2. Carolyn E. Cutrona, *Social Support in Couples: Marriage as a Resource in Times of Stress* (Thousand Oaks, CA: SAGE Publications, 1996).
3. Robert Putnam, "You Gotta Have Friends," *Time* (July 3, 2006): 36.
4. The Barna Group, "Pastors Feel Confident in Ministry, But Many Struggle in their Interaction with Others," *The Barna Update*, July 10, 2006, www.barna.org/FlexPage.aspx?Page=BarnaUpdateNarrow&BarnaUpdateID=242.

5. For more on the subject of family systems and pastoral identity, see Edwin H. Friedman, *Generation to Generation: Family Process in Church and Synagogue* (New York: Guilford Press, 1985) or Ronald W. Richardson, *Creating a Healthier Church: Family Systems Theory, Leadership, and Congregational Life* (Minneapolis: Fortress Press, 1996) and Ronald W. Richardson, *Becoming a Healthier Pastor: Family Systems Theory and the Pastor's Own Family* (Minneapolis: Fortress Press, 2005).

Chapter 5, Relationships in the Family

1. Friedman, *Generation to Generation*.
2. Dan Reiland, "Promises and Pressures: How to Thrive in a Clergy Marriage," *The Pastor's Coach* 4, no. 6 (March 2003). Used by permission. Dr. Dan Reiland's *The Pastor's Coach* is a free monthly e-newsletter available at http://www.injoy.com/Newsletters/pastors/Content/.
3. Cutrona, *Social Support in Couples*, 21.
4. David and Vera Mace, *What's Happening to Clergy Marriages?* (Nashville: Abingdon, 1980), 28.
5. See Howard J. Clinebell and Charlotte H. Clinebell, *The Intimate Marriage* (New York: Harper and Row, 1970).
6. Cited in London and Wiseman, *Pastors at Greater Risk*.
7. Karen Zurheide, "On Being the Other Half," *Rev. Magazine* (2001), www.onlinerev.com.
8. Reiland, "Promises and Pressures: How to Thrive in a Clergy Marriage." Used by permission. Dr. Dan Reiland's *The Pastor's Coach* is a free monthly e-newsletter available at http://www.injoy.com/Newsletters/pastors/Content/.
9. Eric Reed, "Shifting Family Values," *Leadership*, Fall 2006, 38, http://www.christianitytoday.com/le/2006/004/13.35.html.

10. As cited in Thomas F. Coleman, "Drum Roll: New 'Unmarried' Majority Takes Center Stage," Unmarried America, August 21, 2006, http://www.unmarriedamerica.org/column-one/8-21-06-census-release-on-unmarried-majority.htm. U.S. Census Bureau American Community Survey results can be found at http://www.census.gov/acs/www/.
11. William J. Winterrowd, "Being God's Family," *The Living Pulpit* (October-December, 1994): 22.
12. Richardson, *Becoming a Healthier Pastor.*

Chapter 6, Relationships at Church

1. For more on the concept of social capital, see Robert D. Putnam, *Bowling Alone: The Collapse and Revival of American Community* (New York: Simon and Schuster, 2000).
2. Dean R. Hoge and Jacqueline E. Wenger, *Pastors in Transition: Why Clergy Leave Local Church Ministry* (Grand Rapids, MI: William B. Eerdmans Publishing Company, 2005).
3. Chris Turner, "More Than 1,300 Staff Dismissed in 2005; Relationship Issues Again Take First Five Spots," LifeWay Christian Resources, http://www.lifeway.com/lwc/.
4. Fred Oaks, "Four Blunders that Ruin a Pastor-Congregation Partnership," Church Central, http://www.churchcentral.com/nw/s/template/Article.html/id/24090.
5. Chuck Swindoll, "Build Better Relationships with Your Board," Building Church Leaders, 2004, www.BuildingChurchLeaders.com.
6. Bob Wells, "It's Okay to Go There: The Place of Friendship in Ministry," Pulpit and Pew Research on Pastoral Leadership, http://www.pulpitandpew.duke.edu/friendship.htm.
7. Lillian Daniel, "Pastor-Parish Relationships: Can We Be Friends?" *Christian Century*, (June 14, 2005): 26-28.
8. Ronald W. Richardson, *Creating a Healthier Church*, 177.

9. Richardson's book *Creating a Healthier Church* may be help-ful in this process. See also Henry T. Close, "On Saying No to People: A Pastoral Letter," *Journal of Pastoral Care* 28 (1974): 92-98.

10. Thomas F. Fischer, "When Congregational Anxiety Makes Leaders Anxious," *Ministry Health* 340, http://ministryhealth. net/mh_articles/340_cong_anxiety_leaders_anxious.html.

11. Enos Martin and E. A. Vastyan, "Bewildered by the Borderline Personality," *Leadership* (Fall 1989): 42-48.

12. Louis McBurney, "Caring for a Difficult Person," *Building Church Leaders,* http://www.buildingchurchleaders.com/ar-ticles/2006/spiritualcare-howto.html.

13. *Webster's New World College Dictionary, 4th Edition,* s.v. "Pas-sive-aggressive."

14. Barbara Brown Taylor, *Leaving Church: A Memoir of Faith* (San Francisco: HarperSanFrancisco, 2006), 152.

Chapter 7, Relationships in the Community

1. William D. Horton, "The Pastor's Opportunities: II. Commu-nity Involvement," *The Expository Times* 98 (1987). 227-8.

2. Nelson Granade, *Lending Your Leadership: How Pastors Are Redefining Their Role in Community Life* (Herndon, VA: The Alban Institute, 2006).

3. For more information on this interfaith organization, visit their Web site at www.faithtrustinstitute.org.

4. Granade, *Lending Your Leadership*, 65.

5. Jenny Mitchell, e-mail message to author, June 10, 2006.

6. Putnam, *Bowling Alone.*

7. Putnam, *Bowling Alone*, 67.

8. Wells, "It's Okay to Go There: The Place of Friendship in Min-istry."

9. Kinnaman and Ells, *Leaders That Last.*

Chapter 8, Danger!

1. Michael Zigarelli, "The Epidemic of Busyness Among Christian Leaders," *Regent Business Review* 16 (March/April 2005): 3.
2. Zigarelli, "The Epidemic of Busyness Among Christian Leaders," 4.
3. Spaite, *Time Bomb in the Church*.
4. Zigarelli, "The Epidemic of Busyness Among Christian Leaders," 3.
5. Palmer, *Let Your Life Speak*, 49.
6. "Spiritual Leadership: How Can I Possibly Do This Too?" *The Alban Weekly*, (3/21/2005).

Chapter 9, The Care and Feeding of Your Spirit

1. Visit the Web site of the Center for Applications of Psychological Type, www.capt.org, for a complete listing of resources. Earle C. Page has developed a chart, "Finding Your Spiritual Path/ Following Your Spiritual Path," that can be very helpful in understanding one's preferences and needs in the area of spiritual disciplines.
2. Ware, *Discover Your Spiritual Type*.
3. Ruth Haley Barton, *Sacred Rhythms: Arranging Our Lives for Spiritual Transformation* (Downers Grove, IL: InterVarsity Press, 2006); Dallas Willard, *The Spirit of the Disciplines: Understanding How God Changes Lives* (San Francisco: Harper Collins, 1988); Timothy C. Geoffrion, *The Spirit-Led Leader: Nine Leadership Practices and Soul Principles* (Herndon, VA: The Alban Institute, 2005).
4. Trevor Lee, "Fully Present for Prayer," *Christianity Today*. http://www.christianitytoday.com/global/printer.html?/bcl/areas/spiritualgrowth/articles/061206.html.
5. Brother Lawrence, *The Practice of the Presence of God: The Best Rule of a Holy Life* (New York: Fleming H. Revell Co.).

6.   St. Augustine, from Phyllis Tickle, *The Divine Hours: Prayers for Springtime* (New York: Image Books Doubleday, 2001), 134.

7.   W. E. Vine, *An Expository Dictionary of New Testament Words* (Nashville: Thomas Nelson), s.v. "Worship."

8.   Ibid.

9.   Dietrich Bonhoeffer, *Life Together: The Classic Exploration of Faith in Community* (San Francisco: Harper and Row, 1954), 99.

10. Katheryn Rhoads Meek et al, "Maintaining Personal Resiliency: Lessons Learned from Evangelical Protestant Clergy," *Journal of Psychology and Theology* 31: 344.

Chapter 10, Sabbath

1.   Lynne M. Baab, *Sabbath Keeping: Finding Freedom in the Rhythms of Rest* (Downers Grove, IL: InterVarsity Press, 2005), 11.

2.   Spaite, *Time Bomb in the Church.*

3.   Anderson, *The Shape of Practical Theology,* 287.

4.   Eugene H. Peterson, *Working the Angles: The Shape of Pastoral Integrity* (Grand Rapids, MI: William B. Eerdmans Publishing Company, 1987), 72-73.

5.   Wayne Muller, *Sabbath: Finding Rest, Renewal, and Delight in Our Busy Lives* (New York: Bantam Books, 1999), 30.

6.   Peterson, *Working the Angles,* 71.

7.   Muller, *Sabbath,* 31.

8.   Peterson, *Working the Angles,* 73.

9.   Palmer, *Let Your Life Speak,* 30.

10. Peterson, *Working the Angles,* 66.

11. Marva Dawn, *Keeping the Sabbath Wholly: Ceasing, Resting, Embracing, Feasting* (Grand Rapids, MI: William B. Eerdmans Publishing Company, 1989), 34.

Chapter 11, Extended Sabbath Rest

1. Bruce Dyer, "A Review of the Video, *Why You Should Give Your Pastor a Sabbatical* by Roy M. Oswald," presentation to the Professional Effectiveness Committee and the Ministers Council Senate, August 17-21, 2002.

2. "Increasingly, Clergy Seek Sabbaticals for Travel, Study, Reflection and Rest," *Dallas Morning News*, 2006, Red Orbit News, November 15, 2006, http://www.redorbit.com/news/display/?id=731855.

3. Melissa Bane Sevier, *Journeying toward Renewal: A Spiritual Companion for Pastoral Sabbaticals* (Herndon, VA: The Alban Institute, 2002), 10.

4. For more information on the Clergy Renewal Program, go to www.clergyrenewal.org.

5. Tracy Schier, "Clergy Renewal Programs (Part I): Taking Time to Renew Ministerial Vocations," Resources for American Christianity, http://www.resourcingchristianity.org.

6. Terrie Anderson, "Reshaping Ministry in Light of My Sabbatical Experience," Resources for American Christianity (posted 01/01/2005), http://www.resourcingchristianity.org.

7. As quoted in Tracy Schier, "Clergy Renewal Programs (Part II): Renewal is Key to Pastors' Sabbaticals," Resources for American Christianity (posted 09/26/2005), 5, http://www.resourcingchristianity.org.

8. Dyer, 2. Dyer made this suggestion in summarizing and reviewing the video *Why You Should Give Your Pastor a Sabbatical* by Roy M. Oswald.

9. "Increasingly, Clergy Seek Sabbaticals for Travel, Study, Reflection and Rest," *Dallas Morning News*, 2006, Red Orbit News, November 15, 2006, http://www.redorbit.com/news/display/?id=731855.

10. Vincent Rush, "Waiting on Both Halves of the Soul: Ministry as Prose and as Poetry," Resources for American Christianity

(posted 04/24/2005), http://www.resourcingchristianity. org.

11. As quoted in Schier, "Clergy Renewal Programs (Part II), 5.

12. For a listing of pastoral care resources, see Jane Rubietta, "Appendix H" in *How to Keep the Pastor You Love* (Downers Grove, IL: InterVarsity Press, 2002).

13. Schier, "Clergy Renewal Programs (Part II).

Chapter 12, Blessing

1. Cleland B. McAfee, "Near to the Heart of God," *Sing to the Lord* (Kansas City, MO: Lillenas Publishing Company, 1993), 621.

Bibliography

Burnout

Spaite, Daniel. *Time Bomb in the Church: Defusing Pastoral Burnout*. Kansas City, MO: Beacon Hill Press, 1999.

Community Leadership

Granade, Nelson. *Lending Your Leadership: How Pastors Are Redefining Their Role in Community Life*. Herndon, VA: The Alban Institute, 2006.

Covenant Groups

Kinnaman, Gary D., and Alfred H. Ells. *Leaders That Last: How Covenant Friendships Can Help Pastors Thrive*. Grand Rapids, MI: Baker Books, 2003.

Differentiation and Family Systems

Friedman, Edwin H. *Generation to Generation: Family Process in Church and Synagogue*. New York: Guilford, 1985.

Richardson, Ronald W. *Becoming a Healthier Pastor: Family Systems Theory and the Pastor's Own Family*. Minneapolis: Fortress Press, 2005.

Difficult people

Boers, Arthur Paul. *Never Call Them Jerks: Healthy Responses to Difficult Behavior*. Herndon, VA: The Alban Institute, 1999.

Greenfield, Guy. *The Wounded Minister: Healing from and Preventing Personal Attacks*. Grand Rapids, MI: Baker Books, 2001.

Haugk, Kenneth C. *Antagonists in the Church: How to Identify and Deal with Destructive Conflict*. Minneapolis: Augsburg Publishing House, 1988.

Rediger, G. Lloyd. *Clergy Killers: Guidance for Pastors and Congregations Under Attack*. Louisville, KY: Westminster/John Knox, 1997.

Emotional Healing

Smedes, Lewis B. *Shame and Grace: Healing the Shame We Don't Deserve*. San Francisco: HarperCollins, 1993.

Financial Management and Simplicity

Financial Peace University. See www.daveramsey.com.

Linder, Ray. *What Will I Do With My Money? How Your Personality Affects Your Financial Behavior*. Chicago: Northfield Publishing, 2000.

Personality Type

Oswald, Roy M., and Otto Kroeger. *Personality Type and Religious Leadership*. Herndon, VA: The Alban Institute, 1988.

Sabbath and Spiritual Formation

Baab, Lynne M. *Sabbath Keeping: Finding Freedom in the Rhythms of Rest*. Downers Grove, IL: InterVarsity Press, 2005.

Barton, Ruth Haley. *Sacred Rhythms: Arranging Our Lives for Spiritual Transformation*. Downers Grove, IL: InterVarsity Press, 2006.

Geoffrion, Timothy C. *The Spirit-Led Leader: Nine Leadership Practices and Soul Principles*. Herndon, VA: The Alban Institute, 2005.

Muller, Wayne. *Sabbath: Finding Rest, Renewal, and Delight in Our Busy Lives*. New York: Bantam Books, 1999.

Sevier, Melissa Bane. *Journeying toward Renewal: A Spiritual Companion for Pastoral Sabbaticals*. Herndon, VA: The Alban Institute, 2002.

Tickle, Phyllis. *The Divine Hours: Prayers for Springtime*. New York: Image Books Doubleday, 2001.

Ware, Corrine. *Discover Your Spiritual Type: A Guide to Individual and Congregational Growth*. Herndon, VA: The Alban Institute, 1995.